Learning PHP 7
High Performance

Improve the performance of your PHP application
to ensure the application users aren't left waiting

Altaf Hussain

[PACKT] open source ✳

PUBLISHING   community experience distilled

BIRMINGHAM - MUMBAI

Learning PHP 7 High Performance

Copyright © 2016 Packt Publishing

First published: April 2016

Production reference: 1190416

Published by Packt Publishing Ltd.
Livery Place
35 Livery Street
Birmingham B3 2PB, UK.

ISBN 978-1-78588-226-5

www.packtpub.com

Credits

Author
Altaf Hussain

Reviewer
Raul Mesa Ros

Commissioning Editor
Kunal Parikh

Acquisition Editor
Vinay Argekar

Content Development Editor
Priyanka Mehta

Technical Editor
Ravikiran Pise

Copy Editor
Shruti Iyer

Project Coordinator
Izzat Contractor

Proofreader
Safis Editing

Indexer
Rekha Nair

Graphics
Abhinash Sahu

Production Coordinator
Manu Joseph

Cover Work
Manu Joseph

About the Author

Altaf Hussain is a fullstack web and mobile app developer with over 6 years of experience in PHP development. He received his degree in electrical engineering and specialized in computer and communications from Pakistan. Altaf is an electrical engineer on paper and a software engineer by heart.

He worked as a system programmer in his team, developing control software for small test robots using assembly languages and C. After this, Altaf got interested in web technologies and never looked back. He has worked with numerous PHP frameworks, including Zend, Laravel, and Yii, and open source systems such as Drupal, WordPress, PrestaShop, and Magento. Altaf designed and built two proprietary CMS systems with full support for multiple languages and models, permissions, and translations, as well as different kinds of multilingual content management. Now, he works in the fashion industry as the head of IT at shy7lo.com, where his role is to manage the development team on the premises and abroad, in order to manage Magento and Laravel applications development and the deployment life cycle. Besides web apps, Altaf has worked on iOS and Android applications, including building APIs in Lumen. He is a big fan of service-oriented architecture (SOA) and successfully uses it in different applications.

Altaf actively researches on website performance and has deployed the latest technologies, such as PHP 7, NGINX, Redis, Varnish, and others, in production environments for high-speed and scalable applications. He is a Debian lover and uses it for all of his web application deployments.

When not working, Altaf writes articles for `programmingtunes.com` and `techyocean.com`. He has reviewed several books for Packt Publishing, including Learning Phalcon PHP, Mastering jQuery Mobile, and PrestaShop Module Development.

Acknowledgement

I would like to thank my parents, wife, and son, Haashir Khan, who were all very helpful during the development of this book and my overall career. Without their help and support, this book would not have been possible to complete. I would also like to thank the PHP community for creating such awesome and beautiful tools and making the life of a web developer easy.

About the Reviewer

Raul Mesa Ros has been writing software for the Web since 2006. He started with Java, later moved on to PHP, and obtained several certifications such as Zend Engineer and Zend Framework. Having worked on several high-traffic web projects, Raul is nowadays very interested in the DevOps philosophy.

He currently works as a senior web developer at `EuroMillions.com` using DevOps and PHP technologies. Raul also leads various small-to-medium sized projects.

His twitter handle is `@rmrbest`.

I would like to thank my wife, Noemi, and my daughter, Valeria, for their support and love, and also my father who bought me my first computer back in 1992.

www.PacktPub.com

eBooks, discount offers, and more

Did you know that Packt offers eBook versions of every book published, with PDF and ePub files available? You can upgrade to the eBook version at www.PacktPub.com and as a print book customer, you are entitled to a discount on the eBook copy. Get in touch with us at customercare@packtpub.com for more details.

At www.PacktPub.com, you can also read a collection of free technical articles, sign up for a range of free newsletters and receive exclusive discounts and offers on Packt books and eBooks.

https://www2.packtpub.com/books/subscription/packtlib

Do you need instant solutions to your IT questions? PacktLib is Packt's online digital book library. Here, you can search, access, and read Packt's entire library of books.

Why subscribe?

- Fully searchable across every book published by Packt
- Copy and paste, print, and bookmark content
- On demand and accessible via a web browser

Table of Contents

Preface   **vii**

Chapter 1: Setting Up the Environment   **1**

Setting up Windows   **2**
Setting up Debian or Ubuntu   **5**
  Debian   5
  Ubuntu   5
Setting up CentOS   **9**
  Installing NGINX   10
  Installing PHP 7   11
  Installing Percona Server   13
Setting up Vagrant   **14**
Summary   **16**

Chapter 2: New Features in PHP 7   **17**

OOP features   **18**
  Type hints   18
    Scalar type hints   18
    Return type hints   19
  Namespaces and group use declaration   21
    Non mixed group use declarations   25
    Mixed group use declarations   26
    The compound namespace declaration   26
  The anonymous classes   27
  Old-style constructor deprecation   30
  The throwable interface   32
    Error   32
New operators   **33**
  The Spaceship operator (<=>)   33
  The null coalesce operator(??)   35

Uniform variable syntax	**37**
Miscellaneous features and changes	**38**
Constant arrays	38
Multiple default cases in the switch statement	38
The options array for session_start function	39
Filtered unserialize function	39
Summary	**40**
Chapter 3: Improving PHP 7 Application Performance	**41**
NGINX and Apache	**41**
Apache	42
NGINX	42
HTTP server optimization	**43**
Caching static files	43
Apache	43
NGINX	43
HTTP persistent connection	**44**
Apache	45
NGINX	46
GZIP compression	46
Apache	46
NGINX	47
Using PHP as a separate service	48
Disabling unused modules	49
Apache	49
NGINX	50
Web server resources	51
NGINX	51
Content Delivery Network (CDN)	**52**
Using CDN	52
CSS and JavaScript optimization	**54**
Merging	54
Minifying	54
Minify	56
Grunt	58
Full page caching	**62**
Varnish	**63**
The infrastructure	**66**
Web servers	67
The database server	67
Load balancer (LB)	67

HAProxy load balancing   68
  HAProxy installation   68
  HAProxy load balancing   69
Summary   **72**
Chapter 4: Improving Database Performance   **73**
The MySQL database   **73**
  Query caching   74
Storage engines   **75**
  The MyISAM storage engine   76
  The InnoDB storage engine   77
    innodb_buffer_pool_size   77
    innodb_buffer_pool_instances   77
    innodb_log_file_size   78
The Percona Server - a fork of MySQL   **78**
  Installing the Percona Server   78
MySQL performance monitoring tools   **79**
  phpMyAdmin   80
  The MySQL workbench   83
  Percona Toolkit   84
    pt-query-digest   84
    pt-duplicate-key-checker   85
Percona XtraDB Cluster (PXC)   **87**
Redis – the key-value cache store   **89**
  Connecting with the Redis server   92
  Storing and fetching data from the Redis server   92
  Redis management tools   94
Memcached key-value cache store   **95**
Summary   **96**
Chapter 5: Debugging and Profiling   **97**
Xdebug   **97**
  Debugging with Sublime Text   98
  Debugging with Eclipse   102
Profiling with Xdebug   **106**
PHP DebugBar   **107**
Summary   **112**
Chapter 6: Stress/Load Testing PHP Applications   **113**
Apache JMeter   **114**
ApacheBench (ab)   **120**
Siege   **122**

Load testing real-world applications	**124**
Magento 2	125
WordPress 4	126
Drupal 8	127
Summary	**128**
Chapter 7: Best Practices in PHP Programming	**129**
Coding styles	**130**
Test-driven development (TDD)	**133**
Design patterns	**136**
Service-oriented architecture (SOA)	**137**
Being object-oriented and reusable always	**137**
PHP frameworks	**138**
Version control system (VCS) and Git	**138**
Deployment and Continuous Integration (CI)	**138**
Summary	**140**
Appendix A: Tools to Make Life Easy	**141**
Composer – A dependency manager for PHP	**141**
Composer installation	142
Using Composer	142
Git – A version control system	**144**
Git installation	144
Using Git	144
Creating new branches and merging	146
Cloning a repository	148
Webhooks	148
Desktop tools to manage repositories	150
Grunt watch	**151**
Summary	**154**
Appendix B: MVC and Frameworks	**155**
The MVC design pattern	**156**
Model	156
Views	157
Controllers	157
Laravel	**158**
Installation	158
Features	158
Routing	159

Eloquent ORM   160
Artisan CLI   163
Migrations   164
Blade templates   166
Other features   168
Lumen   **169**
Apigility   **169**
Summary   **176**
Index   **177**

Preface

The PHP community faced a huge problem over decades: performance. No matter how powerful hardware they got, in the end, PHP was a bottleneck in itself. With PHP 5.4.x, 5.5.x, and 5.6.x, PHP's performance started to improve, but still it was a huge problem in high-load applications. The community developed caching tools such as **Alternative PHP Cache** (**APC**) and Zend OpCache, which cached the opcode for high performance, and these tools had a good effect on the performance.

To get rid of the performance issues of PHP, Facebook built their own open source tool called **HHVM** (**HipHop Virtual Machine**). According to their official website, HHVM uses the Just In Time (JIT) compilation to achieve superior performance while maintaining the development flexibility that PHP provides. HHVM had great performance compared to PHP, and it is widely used in production for heavy applications such as Magento.

PHP went to war with HHVM using **PHP Next Generation** (**PHPNG**). The whole purpose of PHPNG is to increase performance and focus on the rewriting and optimization of the Zend engine memory allocation and PHP data types. People around the world started benchmarking PHPNG and HHVM, and according to them, PHPNG was outperforming HHVM.

At last, PHPNG was merged with the master branch of PHP, and after a tremendous amount of optimization and complete rewriting, PHP 7 was released with huge performance improvements. PHP 7 is still not JIT, but its performance is great and similar to HHVM. This is a huge performance increase from the older versions of PHP.

What this book covers

Chapter 1, Setting Up the Environment, covers how to set up different development environments, including the installation of NGINX, PHP 7, and Percona Server on Windows, different Linux distros, and setting up the Vagrant virtual machine for development purposes.

Chapter 2, New Features in PHP 7, covers the major new features introduced in PHP 7, including Type Hints, Group use Declarations, Anonymous classes, and new operators, such as Spaceship operator, Null Coalesce operators, and the Uniform variable syntax.

Chapter 3, Improving PHP 7 Application Performance, covers different techniques to increase and scale a PHP 7 application's performance. In this chapter, we cover optimization of NGINX and Apache, CDN, and CSS/JavaScript, such as merging and minifying them, full-page caching, and installing and configuring Varnish. At last, we discuss an ideal infrastructure setup for application development.

Chapter 4, Improving Database Performance, covers techniques to optimize MySQL and Percona Server configuration for high performance. Also, it covers different tools to monitor the performance of a database. It also covers Memcached and Redis for caching objects.

Chapter 5, Debugging and Profiling, covers debugging and profiling techniques including the use of Xdebug for debugging and profiling, debugging with Sublime Text 3 and Eclipse, and the PHP DebugBar.

Chapter 6, Stress/Load Testing PHP Applications, covers different tools to stress and load test the application. It covers Apache JMeter, ApacheBench, and Siege for load testing. It also covers how to load test different open source systems such as Magento, Drupal, and WordPress on PHP 7 and PHP 5.6, and compares their performance on PHP 7 and PHP 5.6.

Chapter 7, Best Practices in PHP Programming, covers a few best practices for producing quality standard code. It covers coding styles, design patterns, service-oriented architecture, test-driven development, Git, and deployments.

Appendix A, Tools to Make Life Easy, discusses three of these tools in much more detail. The tools we will discuss are Composer, Git, and Grunt watch.

Appendix B, MVC and Frameworks, covers MVC design patterns and the most popular frameworks that are used in PHP development, which include Laravel, Lumen, and Apigility.

What you need for this book

Any hardware specification that is compliant to run the latest versions of the following software should be enough to get through this book:

- Operating systems: Debian or Ubuntu
- Software: NGINX, PHP 7, MySQL, PerconaDB, Redis, Memcached, Xdebug, Apache JMeter, ApacheBench, Siege, and Git

Who this book is for

This book is for those who have basic experience in PHP programming. If you are developing performance-critical applications, then this book is for you.

Conventions

In this book, you will find a number of text styles that distinguish between different kinds of information. Here are some examples of these styles and an explanation of their meaning.

Code words in text, database table names, folder names, filenames, file extensions, pathnames, dummy URLs, user input, and Twitter handles are shown as follows: "We can include other contexts through the use of the `include` directive."

A block of code is set as follows:

```
location ~ \.php$ {
  fastcgi_pass    127.0.0.1:9000;
  fastcgi_param    SCRIPT_FILENAME complete_path_webroot_
    folder$fastcgi_script_name;
  include    fastcgi_params;
}
```

When we wish to draw your attention to a particular part of a code block, the relevant lines or items are set in bold:

```
server {
  ...
  ...
  root html;
  index index.php index.html index.htm;
  ...
```

Any command-line input or output is written as follows:

```
php-cgi -b 127.0.0.1:9000
```

New terms and **important words** are shown in bold. Words that you see on the screen, for example, in menus or dialog boxes, appear in the text like this: "Clicking the **Next** button moves you to the next screen."

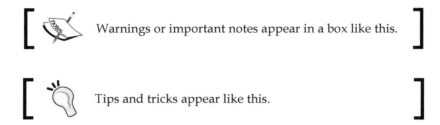

Warnings or important notes appear in a box like this.

Tips and tricks appear like this.

Reader feedback

Feedback from our readers is always welcome. Let us know what you think about this book—what you liked or disliked. Reader feedback is important for us as it helps us develop titles that you will really get the most out of.

To send us general feedback, simply e-mail feedback@packtpub.com, and mention the book's title in the subject of your message.

If there is a topic that you have expertise in and you are interested in either writing or contributing to a book, see our author guide at www.packtpub.com/authors.

Customer support

Now that you are the proud owner of a Packt book, we have a number of things to help you to get the most from your purchase.

Downloading the example code

You can download the example code files for this book from your account at http://www.packtpub.com. If you purchased this book elsewhere, you can visit http://www.packtpub.com/support and register to have the files e-mailed directly to you.

You can download the code files by following these steps:

1. Log in or register to our website using your e-mail address and password.
2. Hover the mouse pointer on the **SUPPORT** tab at the top.
3. Click on **Code Downloads & Errata**.
4. Enter the name of the book in the **Search** box.
5. Select the book for which you're looking to download the code files.
6. Choose from the drop-down menu where you purchased this book from.
7. Click on **Code Download**.

You can also download the code files by clicking on the **Code Files** button on the book's webpage at the Packt Publishing website. This page can be accessed by entering the book's name in the **Search** box. Please note that you need to be logged in to your Packt account.

Once the file is downloaded, please make sure that you unzip or extract the folder using the latest version of:

- WinRAR / 7-Zip for Windows
- Zipeg / iZip / UnRarX for Mac
- 7-Zip / PeaZip for Linux

Downloading the color images of this book

We also provide you with a PDF file that has color images of the screenshots/diagrams used in this book. The color images will help you better understand the changes in the output. You can download this file from `https://www.packtpub.com/sites/default/files/downloads/LearningPHP7HighPerformance_ColorImages.pdf`.

Errata

Although we have taken every care to ensure the accuracy of our content, mistakes do happen. If you find a mistake in one of our books—maybe a mistake in the text or the code—we would be grateful if you could report this to us. By doing so, you can save other readers from frustration and help us improve subsequent versions of this book. If you find any errata, please report them by visiting `http://www.packtpub.com/submit-errata`, selecting your book, clicking on the **Errata Submission Form** link, and entering the details of your errata. Once your errata are verified, your submission will be accepted and the errata will be uploaded to our website or added to any list of existing errata under the Errata section of that title.

To view the previously submitted errata, go to https://www.packtpub.com/books/content/support and enter the name of the book in the search field. The required information will appear under the **Errata** section.

Piracy

Piracy of copyrighted material on the Internet is an ongoing problem across all media. At Packt, we take the protection of our copyright and licenses very seriously. If you come across any illegal copies of our works in any form on the Internet, please provide us with the location address or website name immediately so that we can pursue a remedy.

Please contact us at copyright@packtpub.com with a link to the suspected pirated material.

We appreciate your help in protecting our authors and our ability to bring you valuable content.

Questions

If you have a problem with any aspect of this book, you can contact us at questions@packtpub.com, and we will do our best to address the problem.

Setting Up the Environment

1

PHP 7 has finally been released. For a long time, the PHP community was talking about it and has still not stopped. The main improvement in PHP 7 is its performance. For a long time, the PHP community faced performance issues in large-scale applications. Even some small applications with high traffic faced performance issues. Server resources were increased, but it did not help much because in the end the bottleneck was PHP itself. Different caching techniques were used, such as APC, and this helped a little. However, the community still needed a version of PHP that could boost the application's performance at its peak. And this is where PHPNG comes in.

PHPNG stands for **PHP next generation**. It is a completely separate branch and is mainly targeted for performance. Some people thought that PHPNG is **JIT (Just In Time)** compilation, but in reality, PHPNG is based on a refactored **Zend Engine**, which was highly optimized for performance. PHPNG is used as a base for PHP 7 development, and according to the official PHP wiki page, the PHPNG branch is now merged into the master branch.

Before starting to build an application, the development environment should be finalized and configured. In this chapter, we will discuss setting up the development environment on different systems, such as Windows and different flavors of Linux.

We will cover the following topics:

- Setting up Windows
- Setting up Ubuntu or Debian
- Setting up CentOS
- Setting up Vagrant

All other environments can be skipped, and we can set up the environment that we will use.

Setting up Windows

There are many tools available that have Apache, PHP, and MySQL bundled for Windows, provide easy installation, and are very easy to use. Most of these tools already provide support for PHP 7 with Apache, such as through XAMPP, WAMPP, and EasyPHP. EasyPHP is the only one that also provides support for **NGINX** and provides easy steps to changes webserver from NGINX to Apache or Apache to Nginx.

> XAMPP is also available for Linux and Mac OS X. However, WAMP and EasyPHP are only available for Windows. Any of these three can be used for this book, but we recommend EasyPHP as it supports NGINX, and for this book, we mostly use NGINX.

Any of the three tools can be used, but we require more control over every element of our web server tools, so we will also install NGINX, PHP 7, and MySQL individually and then connect them together.

> NGINX Windows binaries can be downloaded from http://nginx.org/en/download.html. We recommend using a stable version, though there is no problem with using a mainline version. PHP Windows binaries can be downloaded from http://windows.php.net/download/. Download either 32-bit or 64-bit binaries of the *non-thread safe* version according to your system.

Perform the following steps:

1. Download NGINX and PHP Windows binaries mentioned in the information box. Copy NGINX to a suitable directory. For example, we have a completely separate D drive for development purposes. Copy NGINX to this development drive or any other directory. Now, copy PHP either to the NGINX directory or to any other secure folder location.

2. In the PHP directory, there will be two .ini files, php.ini-development and php.ini-production. Rename either one of them to php.ini. PHP will be using this configuration file.

3. Hold the *Shift* key and right click in the PHP directory to open the command-line window. The command-line window will be opened in the same location path. Issue the following command to start PHP:

```
php-cgi -b 127.0.0.1:9000
```

The -b option starts PHP and binds to the path for external **FastCGI** servers. The preceding command binds PHP to loop back the 127.0.0.1 IP on port 9000. Now, PHP is accessible on this path.

4. To configure NGINX, open the nginx_folder/conf/nginx.conf file. The first thing to do is to add root and index to the server block, as follows:

```
server {
    root html;
    index index.php index.html index.htm;
```

> **Downloading the example code**
>
> You can download the example code files for this book from your account at http://www.packtpub.com. If you purchased this book elsewhere, you can visit http://www.packtpub.com/support and register to have the files e-mailed directly to you.
>
> You can download the code files by following these steps:
>
> - Log in or register to our website using your e-mail address and password.
> - Hover the mouse pointer on the SUPPORT tab at the top.
> - Click on Code Downloads & Errata.
> - Enter the name of the book in the Search box.
> - Select the book for which you're looking to download the code files.
> - Choose from the drop-down menu where you purchased this book from.
> - Click on Code Download.
>
> Once the file is downloaded, please make sure that you unzip or extract the folder using the latest version of:
> - WinRAR / 7-Zip for Windows
> - Zipeg / iZip / UnRarX for Mac
> - 7-Zip / PeaZip for Linux

5. Now, we need to configure NGINX to use PHP as FastCGI on the path mentioned before on which it is started. In the nginx.conf file, uncomment the following location block for PHP:

```
location ~ \.php$ {
    fastcgi_pass    127.0.0.1:9000;
```

```
    fastcgi_param    SCRIPT_FILENAME complete_path_webroot_
folder$fastcgi_script_name;
include    fastcgi_params;
}
```

Note the `fastcgi_param` option. The highlighted `complete_path_webroot_folder` path should be the absolute path to the HTML directory inside the `nginx` folder. Let's say that your NGINX is placed at the `D:\nginx` path; then, the absolute path to the HTML folder will be `D:\nginx\html`. However, for the preceding `fastcgi_param` option, `\` should be replaced by `/`.

6. Now, restart NGINX by issuing the following command in the root of the NGINX folder:

    nginx -s restart

7. After NGINX is restarted, open your browser and enter the IP or hostname of your Windows server or machine, and we will see the NGINX welcome message.

8. Now, to verify the PHP installation and its working with NGINX, create an `info.php` file in webroot and enter the following code in it:

    ```php
    <?php
      phpinfo();
    ?>
    ```

9. Now, in the browser, access `your_ip/info.php`, and we will be presented with a page full of PHP and server information. Congratulations! We configured NGINX and PHP to work perfectly together.

On Windows and Mac OS X, we recommend that you use a virtual machine installed with all the tools on a Linux flavor to get the best performance out of the server. It is easy to manage everything in Linux. There are vagrant boxes available that have everything ready to use. Also, a custom virtual machine configuration with all the tools, including NGINX, Apache, PHP 7, Ubuntu, Debian, or CentOS, and other great ones, can be made at `https://puphpet.com`, which is an easy-to-use GUI. Another nice tool is Laravel Homestead, which is a **Vagrant** box with great tools.

Setting up Debian or Ubuntu

Ubuntu is derived from Debian, so the process is the same for both Ubuntu and Debian. We will use Debian 8 Jessie and Ubuntu 14.04 Server LTS. The same process can be applied to desktop versions for both.

First, add the repositories for both Debian and Ubuntu.

Debian

As of the time we're writing this book, Debian does not provide an official repository for PHP 7. So, for Debian, we will use dotdeb repositories to install NGINX and PHP 7. Perform the following steps:

1. Open the /etc/apt/sources.list file and add the following two lines at the end of the file:

   ```
   deb http://packages.dotdeb.org jessie all
   deb-src http://packages.dotdeb.org jessie all
   ```

2. Now, execute the following commands in the terminal:

   ```
   wget https://www.dotdeb.org/dotdeb.gpg

   sudo apt-key add dotdeb.gpg

   sudo apt-get update
   ```

The first two commands will add dotdeb repo to Debian and the last command will refresh the cache for sources.

Ubuntu

As of the time of writing this book, Ubuntu also does not provide PHP 7 in their official repos, so we will use a third-party repo for the PHP 7 installation. Perform the following steps:

1. Run the following commands in the terminal:

   ```
   sudo add-apt-repository ppa:ondrej/php

   sudo apt-get update
   ```

2. Now, the repositories are added. Let's install NGINX and PHP 7.

> The rest of the process is mostly the same for both Debian and Ubuntu, so we wont list them separately, as we did for the adding repositories section.

3. To install NGINX, run the following command in the terminal (Debian and Ubuntu):

```
sudo apt-get install nginx
```

4. After the installation is successful, it can be verified by entering the hostname and IP of the Debian or Ubuntu server. If we see something similar to the following screenshot, then our installation is successful:

Welcome to nginx on Debian!

If you see this page, the nginx web server is successfully installed and working on Debian. Further configuration is required.

For online documentation and support please refer to nginx.org

Please use the `reportbug` tool to report bugs in the nginx package with Debian. However, check existing bug reports before reporting a new bug.

Thank you for using debian and nginx.

The following is a list of three useful NGINX commands:

- `service nginx start`: This starts the NGINX server
- `service nginx restart`: This restarts the NGINX server
- `service nginx stop`: This stops the NGINX server

5. Now, it's time to install PHP 7 by issuing the following command:

```
sudo apt-get install php7.0 php7.0-fpm php7.0-mysql php7.0-mcrypt
php7.0-cli
```

This will install PHP 7 along with the other modules mentioned. Also, we installed PHP Cli for the command-line purpose. To verify whether PHP 7 is properly installed, issue the following command in the terminal:

```
php -v
```

6. If it displays the PHP version along with some other details, as shown in the following screenshot, then PHP is properly installed:

```
~ # php -v
PHP 7.0.3-1~dotdeb+8.1 (cli) ( NTS )
Copyright (c) 1997-2016 The PHP Group
Zend Engine v3.0.0, Copyright (c) 1998-2016 Zend Technologies
    with Zend OPcache v7.0.6-dev, Copyright (c) 1999-2016, by Zend Technologies
~ #
```

7. Now, we need to configure NGINX to work with PHP 7. First, copy the
    NGINX default config file `/etc/nginx/sites-available/default` to
    `/etc/nginx/sites-available/www.packt.com.conf` using the following
    command in the terminal:

    ```
    cd /etc/nginx/sites-available

    sudo cp default www.packt.com.conf

    sudo ln -s /etc/nginx /sites-available/www.packt.com.conf /etc/
    nginx/sites-enabled/www.packt.com.conf
    ```

    First, we copied the default configuration file, created another virtual host
    configuration file, `www.packt.com.conf`, and then created a symbolic link
    file to this virtual host file in the sites-enabled folder.

     It is good practice to create a configuration file for each virtual
    host by the same name as of the domain so that it can easily be
    recognized by any other person.

8. Now, open the `/etc/nginx/sites-available/www.packt.com.conf` file
    and add or edit the highlighted code, as shown here:

    ```
    server {
      server_name your_ip:80;
      root /var/www/html;
      index index.php index.html index.htm;
      location ~ \.php$ {
        fastcgi_pass unix:/var/run/php/php7.0-fpm.sock;
          fastcgi_index index.php;
          include fastcgi_params;
      }
    }
    ```

    The preceding configuration is not a complete configuration file. We copied
    only those configuration options that are important and that we may want
    to change.

    In the preceding code, our webroot path is `/var/www/html`, where our PHP
    files and other application files will be placed. In the index config option,
    add `index.php` so that if no file is provided in the URL, NGINX can look
    for and parse `index.php`.

    We added a location block for PHP that includes a `fastcgi_pass` option,
    which has a path to the PHP7 FPM socket. Here, our PHP runs on a Unix
    socket, which is faster than that of TCP/IP.

9. After making these changes, restart NGINX. Now, to test whether PHP and NGINX are properly configured, create an `info.php` file at the root of the `webroot` folder and place the following code in it:

```php
<?php
  phpinfo();
  ?>
```

10. Now, in the browser, type `server_ip/info.php`, and if you see a PHP configuration page, then congratulations! PHP and NGINX are both properly configured.

 If PHP and NGINX run on the same system, then PHP listens to the loopback IP at port `9000`. The port can be changed to any other port. In case, we want to run PHP on the TCP/IP port, then in `fastcgi_pass`, we will enter `127.0.0.1:9000`.

Now, let's install **Percona Server**. Percona Server is a fork of MySQL and is optimized for high performance. We will read more about Percona Server in *Chapter 3, Increasing PHP 7 Application Performance*. Now, let's install Percona Server on Debian/Ubuntu via the following steps:

1. First, let's add the Percona Server repository to our system by running the following command in the terminal:

```
sudo wget https://repo.percona.com/apt/percona-release_0.1-
3.$(lsb_release -sc)_all.deb
sudo dpkg -i percona-release_0.1-3.$(lsb_release -sc)_all.deb
```

The first command will download the repo packages from the Percona repo. The second command will install the downloaded packages and will create a `percona-release.list` file at `/etc/apt/sources.list.d/percona-release.list`.

2. Now, install Percona Server by executing the following command in the terminal:

```
sudo apt-get update
```

3. Now, issue the following command to install Percona Server:

```
sudo apt-get install percona-server-5.5
```

The installation process will start. It will take a while to download it.

For the purpose of this book, we will install Percona Server 5.5. Percona Server 5.6 is also available, which can be installed without any issues.

During the installation, the password for the `root` user will be asked, as shown in the following screenshot:

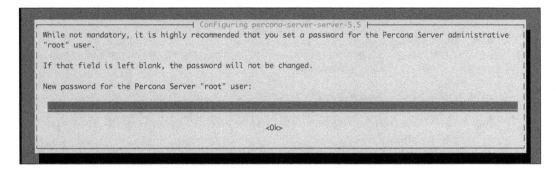

It is optional but recommended to enter the password. After entering the password, re-enter the password on the next screen. The installation process will continue.

4. After the installation is complete, the Percona Server installation can be verified by using the following command:

```
mysql --version
```

It will display the version of Percona Server. As mentioned before, Percona Server is a fork of MySQL, so all the same MySQL commands, queries, and settings can be used.

Setting up CentOS

CentOS is a fork of **Red Hat Enterprise Linux** (**RHEL**) and stands for **Community Enterprise Operating System**. It is a widely used OS on servers specially used by hosting companies to provide shared hosting.

Let's start by configuring CentOS for our development environment. Perform the following steps:

Installing NGINX

1. First, we need to add NGINX RPM to our CentOS installation because CentOS does not provide any default repository for NGINX. Issue the following command in your terminal:

   ```
   sudo rpm -Uvh
   http://nginx.org/packages/centos/7/noarch/RPMS/nginx-release-
   centos-7-0.el7.ngx.noarch.rpm
   ```

   This will add the NGINX repo to CentOS.

2. Now, issue the following command to see which versions of NGINX are available to install:

   ```
   sudo yum --showduplicates list Nginx
   ```

   This will show you the latest stable releases. In our case, it displays NGINX 1.8.0 and NGINX 1.8.1.

3. Now, let's install NGINX using the following command:

   ```
   sudo yum install Nginx
   ```

   This will install NGINX.

4. On CentOS, NGINX won't start automatically after installation or restarting. So, first, we will enable NGINX to autostart after a system restarts using the following command:

   ```
   systemctl enable Nginx.service
   ```

5. Now, let's start NGINX by issuing the following command:

   ```
   systemctl start Nginx.service
   ```

6. Then, open your browser and enter the IP of the CentOS server or host name. If you see the same welcome screen as we saw in the figure earlier in the chapter for Debian, then NGINX is installed successfully.

   To check which version of NGINX is installed, issue the following command in the terminal:

   ```
   Nginx -v
   ```

   On our server, the NGINX version installed is 1.8.1.

   Now, our web server is ready.

Installing PHP 7

1. The next step is to install PHP 7 FPM and configure both NGINX and PHP 7 to work together. As of the time of writing this book, PHP 7 is not packaged in official CentOS repositories. So, we have two choices to install PHP 7: either we build it from source, or we use third-party repositories. Building from source is a little bit difficult, so let's go the easy way and use third-party repositories.

 For this book, we will use webtatic repos for the PHP 7 installation as they provide quick updates for the new versions. There are some more repositories, and it is just the reader's choice to use any repository as long as it works.

2. Now, let's add a webtatic repository to our CentOS repo by issuing the following command:

   ```
   rpm -Uvh https://dl.fedoraproject.org/pub/epel/epel-release-latest-7.noarch.rpm
   ```

   ```
   rpm -Uvh https://mirror.webtatic.com/yum/el7/webtatic-release.rpm
   ```

3. After the repos are added successfully, issue the following command to see which version is available for installation:

   ```
   sudo yum -showduplicates list php70w
   ```

   In our case, PHP 7.0.3 is available to install.

4. Now, issue the following command to install PHP 7 along with some modules that may be required:

   ```
   sudo yum install php70w php70w-common php70w-cli php70w-fpm php70w-mysql php70w-opcache php70w-mcrypt
   ```

5. This will install core PHP 7 and some modules available for PHP 7. If any other module is required, it can be installed easily; however, first, search to check whether it is available or not. Issue the following command in the terminal to see all the available modules for PHP 7:

   ```
   sudo yum search php70w-
   ```

   We will see a long list of all the available modules for PHP 7.

6. Now, let's say that we want to install the PHP 7 gd module; issue the following command:

   ```
   sudo yum install php70w-gd
   ```

This will install the gd module. Multiple modules can be installed using the same command and separating each module by a space, as we did in the initial installation of PHP.

Now, to check which version of PHP is installed, issue the following command:

`php -v`

In our case, PHP 7.0.3 is installed.

7. To start, stop, and restart PHP, issue the following commands in the terminal:

```
sudo systemctl start php-fpm

sudo systemctl restart php-fpm

sudo systemctl stop php-fpm
```

8. Now, let's configure NGINX to use PHP FPM. Open the default NGINX virtual host file located at /etc/Nginx/conf.d/default.conf using either vi, nano, or any other editor of your choice. Now, make sure that two options are set in the server block, as follows:

```
server {
    listen  80;
    server_name  localhost;
    root    /usr/share/nginx/html;
index  index.php index.html index.htm;
```

The root option indicates the web document root where our website source code files will be placed. Index indicates the default files that will be loaded along with extensions. If any of these files are found, they will be executed by default, regardless of any file mentioned in the URLs.

9. The next configuration in NGINX is a location block for PHP. The following is the configuration for PHP:

```
location ~ \.php$ {
    try_files $uri =404;
    fastcgi_split_path_info ^(.+\.php)(/.+)$;
    fastcgi_pass 127.0.0.1:9000;
    fastcgi_index index.php;
    fastcgi_param SCRIPT_FILENAME
      $document_root$fastcgi_script_name;
      include fastcgi_params;
    }
```

The preceding block is the most important configuration as it enables NGINX to communicate with PHP. The line `fastcgi_pass 127.0.0.1:9000` tells NGINX that PHP FPM can be accessed on the `127.0.0.1` loopback IP on port `9000`. The rest of the details are the same as those we discussed for Debian and Ubuntu.

10. Now, to test our installation, we will create a file named `info.php` with the following contents:

```
<?php
  phpinfo();
?>
```

After saving the file, type `http://server_ip/info.php` or `http://hostname/info.php`, and we will get a page with complete information about PHP. If you see this page, congratulations! PHP runs alongside NGINX.

Installing Percona Server

1. Now, we will install Percona Server on CentOS. The installation process is the same, except that it has a separate repository. To add the Percona Server repo to CentOS, execute the following command in the terminal:

```
sudo yum install http://www.percona.com/downloads/
percona-release/redhat/0.1-3/percona-release-0.1-3.noarch.rpm
```

After the repo installation is completed, a message will be displayed stating the completion of the installation.

2. Now, to test the repo, issue the following command, and it will list all the available Percona packages:

```
sudo yum search percona
```

3. To install Percona Server 5.5, issue the following command in the terminal:

```
sudo yum install Percona-Server-server-55
```

The installation process will start. The rest of the process is the same as for Debian/Ubuntu.

4. After the installation is completed, we will see a completion message.

Setting up Vagrant

Vagrant is a tool used by developers for development environments. Vagrant provides an easy command-line interface to set up virtual machines with all the tools required. Vagrant uses boxes called Vagrant Boxes that can have a Linux operating system and other tools according to this box. Vagrant supports both Oracle VM VirtualBox and VMware. For the purpose of this book, we will use VirtualBox, which we assume is installed on your machine as well.

Vagrant has several boxes for PHP 7, including Laravel Homestead and Rasmus PHP7dev. So, let's get started by configuring the Rasmus PHP7dev box on Windows and Mac OS X.

 We assume that both VirutalBox and Vagrant are installed on our machine. VirtualBox can be downloaded from `https://www.virtualbox.org/wiki/Downloads`, and Vagrant can be downloaded from `https://www.vagrantup.com/downloads.html` for different platforms. Details about Rasmus PHP7dev VagrantBox can be found at `https://github.com/rlerdorf/php7dev`.

Perform the following steps:

1. Make a directory in one of the drives. For example, we made a `php7` directory in our D drive. Then, open the command line in this specific folder directly by holding the *Shift* key, right-clicking, and then selecting **Open command window here**.

2. Now, issue the following command in the command window:

    ```
    vagrant box add rasmus/php7dev
    ```

    It will start downloading the Vagrant box, as shown in the following screenshot:

```
vagrant box add rasmus/php7dev

D:\php7>vagrant box add rasmus/php7dev
==> box: Loading metadata for box 'rasmus/php7dev'
    box: URL: https://atlas.hashicorp.com/rasmus/php7dev
==> box: Adding box 'rasmus/php7dev' (v0.1.0) for provider: virtualbox
    box: Downloading: https://atlas.hashicorp.com/rasmus/boxes/php7dev/versions/0.1.0/providers/virtualbox.box
    box: Progress: 1% (Rate: 511k/s, Estimated time remaining: 1:50:28)))
```

3. Now, when the download is completed, we need to initialize it so that the box is configured and added to VirtualBox for us. Issue the following command in the command window:

```
vagrant init rasmus/php7dev
```

This will start adding the box to VirtualBox and configuring it. When the process is completed, it will display a message, as in the following screenshot:

```
D:\php7>vagrant init rasmus/php7dev
A `Vagrantfile` has been placed in this directory. You are now
ready to `vagrant up` your first virtual environment! Please read
the comments in the Vagrantfile as well as documentation on
`vagrantup.com` for more information on using Vagrant.

D:\php7>
```

4. Now, issue the following command, which will completely set up the Vagrant box and start it up and running:

```
vagrant up
```

This process will take a little bit of time. When it is completed, your box is ready and running and can be used.

5. Now, the first thing to do after it is up is to update everything. This box uses Ubuntu, so open the command window in the same php7dev directory and issue the following command:

```
vagrant ssh
```

It will connect us with the virtual machines through SSH.

 In Windows, if SSH in not installed or not configured in the PATH variable, PuTTY can be used. It can be downloaded from http://www.chiark.greenend.org.uk/~sgtatham/putty/download.html. For PuTTY, the host will be 127.0.0.1, and the port will be 2222. Vagrant is both the username and password for SSH.

6. When we are logged in to the box OS, issue the following commands to update the system:

```
sudo apt-get update
```

```
sudo apt-get upgrade
```

This will update the core system, NGINX, MySQL, PHP 7, and other installed tools if new versions are available.

7. The box is now ready to use for development purposes. The box can be accessed in the browser by typing its IP address in the browser window. To find the IP address of the box, issue the following command in the SSH-connected command window:

```
sudo ifconfig
```

This will display some details. Find out the IPv4 details there and take the IP of the box.

Summary

In this chapter, we configured different environments for the purpose of development. We installed NGINX and PHP 7 on the windows machine. We also configured Debian/Ubuntu and installed NGINX, PHP, and Percona Server 5.5. Then, we configured CentOS and installed NGINX, PHP, and Percona Server 5.5. Lastly, we discussed how to configure Vagrant Box on a Windows machine.

In the next chapter, we will study new features in PHP 7, such as type hints, namespace groupings and declarations, the Spaceship operator, and other features.

2
New Features in PHP 7

PHP 7 has introduced new features that can help programmers write high-performing and effective code. Also, some old-fashioned features are completely removed, and PHP 7 will throw an error if used. Most of the fatal errors are now exceptions, so PHP won't show an ugly fatal error message any more; instead, it will go through an exception with the available details.

In this chapter, we will cover the following topics:

- Type hints
- Namespaces and group use declarations
- The anonymous classes
- Old-style constructor deprecation
- The Spaceship operator
- The null coalesce operator
- Uniform variable syntax
- Miscellaneous changes

OOP features

PHP 7 introduced a few new OOP features that will enable developers to write clean and effective code. In this section, we will discuss these features.

Type hints

Prior to PHP 7, there was no need to declare the data type of the arguments passed to a function or class method. Also, there was no need to mention the return data type. Any data type can be passed to and returned from a function or method. This is one of the huge problems in PHP, in which it is not always clear which data types should be passed or received from a function or method. To fix this problem, PHP 7 introduced type hints. As of now, two type hints are introduced: scalar and return type hints. These are discussed in the following sections.

Type hints is a feature in both OOP and procedural PHP because it can be used for both procedural functions and object methods.

Scalar type hints

PHP 7 made it possible to use scalar type hints for integers, floats, strings, and Booleans for both functions and methods. Let's have a look at the following example:

```php
class Person
{
  public function age(int $age)
  {
    return $age;
    }

  public function name(string $name)
  {
    return $name;
    }

  public function isAlive(bool $alive)
  {
    return $alive;
    }

}

$person = new Person();
echo $person->name('Altaf Hussain');
echo $person->age(30);
echo $person->isAlive(TRUE);
```

In the preceding code, we created a `Person` class. We have three methods, and each method receives different arguments whose data types are defined with them, as is highlighted in the preceding code. If you run the preceding code, it will work fine as we will pass the desired data types for each method.

Age can be a float, such as `30.5` years; so, if we pass a float number to the `age` method, it will still work, as follows:

```
echo $person->age(30.5);
```

Why is that? It is because, by default, *scalar type hints are nonrestrictive*. This means that we can pass float numbers to a method that expects an integer number.

To make it more restrictive, the following single-line code can be placed at the top of the file:

```
declare(strict_types = 1);
```

Now, if we pass a float number to the `age` function, we will get an **Uncaught Type Error**, which is a fatal error that tells us that `Person::age` must be of the int type given the float. Similar errors will be generated if we pass a string to a method that is not of the string type. Consider the following example:

```
echo $person->isAlive('true');
```

The preceding code will generate the fatal error as the string is passed to it.

Return type hints

Another important feature of PHP 7 is the ability to define the return data type for a function or method. It behaves the same way scalar type hints behave. Let's modify our `Person` class a little to understand return type hints, as follows:

```
class Person
{
  public function age(float $age) : string
  {
    return 'Age is '.$age;
  }

  public function name(string $name) : string
  {
    return $name;
    }
```

```php
  public function isAlive(bool $alive) : string
  {
    return ($alive) ? 'Yes' : 'No';
  }

}
```

The changes in the class are highlighted. The return type is defined using the : data-type syntax. It does not matter if the return type is the same as the scalar type. These can be different as long as they match their respective data types.

Now, let's try an example with the object return type. Consider the previous Person class and add a getAddress method to it. Also, we will add a new class, Address, to the same file, as shown in the following code:

```php
class Address
{
  public function getAddress()
  {
  return ['street' => 'Street 1', 'country' => 'Pak'];
  }
}

class Person
{
  public function age(float $age) : string
  {
    return 'Age is '.$age;
  }

  public function name(string $name) : string
  {
    return $name;
  }

  public function isAlive(bool $alive) : string
  {
    return ($alive) ? 'Yes' : 'No';
  }

  public function getAddress() : Address
  {
  return new Address();
  }
}
```

The additional code added to the `Person` class and the new `Address` class is highlighted. Now, if we call the `getAddress` method of the `Person` class, it will work perfectly and won't throw an error. However, let's suppose that we change the return statement, as follows:

```
public function getAddress() : Address
{
   return ['street' => 'Street 1', 'country' => 'Pak'];
}
```

In this case, the preceding method will throw an *uncaught* exception similar to the following:

```
Fatal error: Uncaught TypeError: Return value of Person::getAddress()
must be an instance of Address, array returned
```

This is because we return an array instead of an `Address` object. Now, the question is: why use type hints? The big advantage of using type hints is that it will always avoid accidentally passing or returning wrong and unexpected data to methods or functions.

As can be seen in the preceding examples, this makes the code clear, and by looking at the declarations of the methods, one can exactly know which data types should be passed to each of the methods and what kind of data is returned by looking into the code of each method or comment, if any.

Namespaces and group use declaration

In a very large codebase, classes are divided into namespaces, which makes them easy to manage and work with. However, if there are too many classes in a namespace and we need to use 10 of them, then we have to type the complete use statement for all these classes.

In PHP, it is not required to divide classes in subfolders according to their namespace, as is the case with other programming languages. Namespaces just provide a logical separation of classes. However, we are not limited to placing our classes in subfolders according to our namespaces.

For example, we have a `Publishers/Packt` namespace and the classes `Book`, `Ebook`, `Video`, and `Presentation`. Also, we have a `functions.php` file, which has our normal functions and is in the same `Publishers/Packt` namespace. Another file, `constants.php`, has the constant values required for the application and is in the same namespace. The code for each class and the `functions.php` and `constants.php` files is as follows:

```php
//book.php
namespace Publishers\Packt;

class Book
{
  public function get() : string
  {
    return get_class();
  }
}
```

Now, the code for the `Ebook` class is as follows:

```php
//ebook.php
namespace Publishers\Packt;

class Ebook
{
  public function get() : string
  {
    return get_class();
  }
}
```

The code for the `Video` class is as follows:

```php
//presentation.php
namespace Publishers\Packt;

class Video
{
  public function get() : string
  {
    return get_class();
  }
}
```

Similarly, the code for the presentation class is as follows:

```php
//presentation.php
namespace Publishers\Packt;

class Presentation
{
  public function get() : string
  {
    return get_class();
  }
}
```

All the four classes have the same methods, which return the classes' names using the PHP built-in get_class() function.

Now, add the following two functions to the functions.php file:

```php
//functions.php

namespace Publishers\Packt;

function getBook() : string
{
  return 'PHP 7';
}
function saveBook(string $book) : string
{
  return $book.' is saved';
}
```

Now, let's add the following code to the constants.php file:

```php
//constants.php

namespace Publishers/Packt;

const COUNT = 10;
const KEY = '123DGHtiop09847';
const URL = 'https://www.Packtpub.com/';
```

The code in both functions.php and constants.php is self-explanatory. Note that each file has a namespace Publishers/Packt line at the top, which makes these classes, functions, and constants belong to this namespace.

Now, there are three ways to use the classes, functions, and constants. Let's consider each one.

Take a look at the following code:

```
//Instantiate objects for each class in namespace

$book = new Publishers\Packt\Book();
$ebook = new Publishers\Packt\Ebook();
$video = new Publishers\Packt\Video();
$presentation = new Publishers\Packt\Presentation();

//Use functions in namespace

echo Publishers/Packt/getBook();
echo Publishers/Packt/saveBook('PHP 7 High Performance');

//Use constants

echo Publishers\Packt\COUNT;
echo Publishers\Packt\KEY;
```

In the preceding code, we used namespace names directly while creating objects or using functions and constants. The code looks fine, but it is cluttered. Namespace is everywhere, and if we have lots of namespaces, it will look very ugly, and the readability will be affected.

 We did not include class files in the previous code. Either the include statements or PHP's __autoload function can be used to include all the files.

Now, let's rewrite the preceding code to make it more readable, as follows:

```
use Publishers\Packt\Book;
use Publishers\Packt\Ebook;
use Publishers\Packt\Video;
use Publishers\Packt\Presentation;
use function Publishers\Packt\getBook;
use function Publishers\Packt\saveBook;
use const Publishers\Packt\COUNT;
use const Publishers\Packt\KEY;

$book = new Book();
$ebook = new Ebook(();
```

```
$video = new Video();
$pres = new Presentation();

echo getBook();
echo saveBook('PHP 7 High Performance');

echo COUNT;
echo KEY;
```

In the preceding code, at the top, we used PHP statements for specific classes, functions, and constants in a namespace. However, we still wrote duplicate lines of code for each class, function, and/or constant. This may lead to us have lots of use statements at the top of the file, and the overall verbosity would not be good.

To fix this problem, PHP 7 introduced group use declaration. There are three types of group use declarations:

- Non mixed use declarations
- Mixed use declarations
- Compound use declarations

Non mixed group use declarations

Consider that we have different types of features in a namespace, as we have classes, functions, and contacts in a namespace. In non mixed group use declarations, we declare them separately using a use statement. To better understand it, take a look at the following code:

```
use Publishers\Packt\{ Book, Ebook, Video, Presentation };
use function Publishers\Packt\{ getBook, saveBook };
use const Publishers\Packt\{ COUNT, KEY };
```

We have three types of features in a namespace: class, functions, and constants. So, we have used separate group use declaration statements to use them. The code is now looking more cleaner, organized, and readable and doesn't require too much duplicate typing.

Mixed group use declarations

In this declaration, we combine all types into a single `use` statement. Take a look at the following code:

```
use Publishers\Packt\{
  Book,
  Ebook,
  Video,
  Presentation,
  function getBook,
  function saveBook,
  const COUNT,
  const KEY
};
```

The compound namespace declaration

To understand the compound namespace declaration, we will consider the following criteria.

Let's say we have a `Book` class in the `Publishers\Packt\Paper` namespace. Also, we have an `Ebook` class in the `Publishers\Packt\Electronic` namespace. The `Video` and `Presentation` classes are in the `Publishers\Packt\Media` namespace. So, to use these classes, we will use the code, as follows:

```
use Publishers\Packt\Paper\Book;
use Publishers\Packt\Electronic\Ebook;
use Publishers\Packt\Media\{Video,Presentation};
```

In the compound namespace declaration, we can use the preceding namespaces as follows:

```
use Publishers\Packt\{
  Paper\Book,
  Electronic\Ebook,
  Media\Video,
  Media\Presentation
};
```

It is more elegant and clear, and it doesn't require extra typing if the namespace names are long.

The anonymous classes

An anonymous class is a class that is declared and instantiated at the same time. It does not have a name and can have the full features of a normal class. These classes are useful when a single one-time small task is required to be performed and there is no need to write a full-blown class for it.

 While creating an anonymous class, it is not named, but it is named internally in PHP with a unique reference based on its address in the memory block. For example, the internal name of an anonymous class may be `class@0x4f6a8d124`.

The syntax of this class is the same as that of the named classes, but only the name of the class is missing, as shown in the following syntax:

```
new class(argument) { definition };
```

Let's look at a basic and very simple example of an anonymous class, as follows:

```
$name = new class() {
  public function __construct()
  {
    echo 'Altaf Hussain';
  }
};
```

The preceding code will just display the output as `Altaf Hussain`.

Arguments can also be passed to the *anonymous class constructor*, as shown in the following code:

```
$name = new class('Altaf Hussain') {
  public function __construct(string $name)
  {
    echo $name;
  }
};
```

This will give us the same output as the first example.

Anonymous classes can extend other classes and have the same parent-child classes functioning as normal named classes. Let's have another example; take a look at the following:

```
class Packt
{
  protected $number;

  public function __construct()
  {
    echo 'I am parent constructor';
  }

  public function getNumber() : float
  {
    return $this->number;
  }
}

$number = new class(5) extends packt
{
  public function __construct(float $number)
  {
    parent::__construct();
    $this->number = $number;
  }
};

echo $number->getNumber();
```

The preceding code will display I am parent constructor and 5. As can be seen, we extended the Packt class the way we extend named classes. Also, we can access the public and protected properties and methods within the anonymous class and public properties and methods using anonymous class objects.

Anonymous classes can implement interfaces too, the same as named classes. Let's create an interface first. Run the following:

```
interface Publishers
{
  public function __construct(string $name, string $address);
  public function getName();
  public function getAddress();
}
```

Now, let's modify our `Packt` class as follows. We added the highlighted code:

```
class Packt
{
  protected $number;
  protected $name;
  protected $address;
  public function …
}
```

The rest of the code is same as the first `Packt` class. Now, let's create our anonymous class, which will implement the `Publishers` interface created in the previous code and extend the new `Packt` class, as follows:

```
$info = new class('Altaf Hussain', 'Islamabad, Pakistan')
  extends packt implements Publishers
{
  public function __construct(string $name, string $address)
  {
    $this->name = $name;
    $this->address = $address;
  }

  public function getName() : string
  {
  return $this->name;
  }

  public function getAddress() : string
  {
  return $this->address;
  }
}

  echo $info->getName(). ' '.$info->getAddress();
```

The preceding code is self-explanatory and will output `Altaf Hussain` along with the address.

It is possible to use anonymous classes within another class, as shown here:

```
class Math
{
  public $first_number = 10;
  public $second_number = 20;
```

```
    public function add() : float
    {
      return $this->first_number + $this->second_number;
    }

    public function multiply_sum()
    {
      return new class() extends Math
      {
        public function multiply(float $third_number) : float
        {
          return $this->add() * $third_number;
        }
      };
    }
  }

$math = new Math();
echo $math->multiply_sum()->multiply(2);
```

The preceding code will return 60. How does this happen? The Math class has a multiply_sum method that returns the object of an anonymous class. This anonymous class is extended from the Math class and has a multiply method. So, our echo statement can be divided into two parts: the first is $math->multiply_sum(), which returns the object of the anonymous class, and the second is ->multiply(2), in which we chained this object to call the anonymous class's multiply method along with an argument of the value 2.

In the preceding case, the Math class can be called the outer class, and the anonymous class can be called the inner class. However, remember that it is not required for the inner class to extend the outer class. In the preceding example, we extended it just to ensure that the inner classes could have access to the outer classes' properties and methods by extending the outer classes.

Old-style constructor deprecation

Back in PHP 4, the constructor of a class has the same name method as that of the class. It is still used and is valid until PHP's 5.6 version. However, now, in PHP 7, it is deprecated. Let's have an example, as shown here:

```
class Packt
{
  public function packt()
  {
```

```
    echo 'I am an old style constructor';
  }
}

$packt = new Packt();
```

The preceding code will display the output I am an old style constructor with a deprecated message, as follows:

```
Deprecated: Methods with the same name as their class will not be
constructors in a future version of PHP; Packt has a deprecated
constructor in...
```

However, the old style constructor is still called. Now, let's add the PHP __ construct method to our class, as follows:

```
class Packt
{
  public function __construct()
  {
    echo 'I am default constructor';
  }

  public function packt()
  {
    echo 'I am just a normal class method';
  }
}

$packt = new Packt();
$packt->packt();
```

In the preceding code, when we instantiated the object of the class, the normal __ construct constructor was called. The packt() method isn't considered a normal class method.

 Old-style constructors are deprecated, which means that they will still work in PHP 7 and a deprecated message will be displayed, but it will be removed in the upcoming versions. It is best practice to not use them.

The throwable interface

PHP 7 introduced a base interface that can be base for every object that can use the `throw` statement. In PHP, exceptions and errors can occur. Previously, exceptions could be handled, but it was not possible to handle errors, and thus, any fatal error caused the complete application or a part of the application to halt. To make errors (the most fatal errors) catchable as well, PHP 7 introduced the *throwable* interface, which is implemented by both the exception and error.

 The PHP classes we created can't implement the throwable interface. If required, these classes must extend an exception.

We all know exceptions, so in this topic, we will only discuss errors, which can handle the ugly, fatal errors.

Error

Almost all fatal errors can now throw an error instance, and similarly to exceptions, error instances can be caught using the `try/catch` block. Let's have a simple example:

```
function iHaveError($object)
{
  return $object->iDontExist();
  {

//Call the function
iHaveError(null);
echo "I am still running";
```

If the preceding code is executed, a fatal error will be displayed, the application will be halted, and the `echo` statement won't be executed in the end.

Now, let's place the function call in the `try/catch` block, as follows:

```
try
{
  iHaveError(null);
} catch(Error $e)
{
  //Either display the error message or log the error message
  echo $e->getMessage();
}

echo 'I am still running';
```

Now, if the preceding code is executed, the `catch` body will be executed, and after this, the rest of the application will continue running. In the preceding case, the `echo` statement will be executed.

In most cases, the error instance will be thrown for the most fatal errors, but for some errors, a subinstance of error will be thrown, such as `TypeError`, `DivisionByZeroError`, `ParseError`, and so on.

Now, let's take a look at a `DivisionByZeroError` exception in the following example:

```
try
{
  $a = 20;
  $division = $a / 20;
} catch(DivisionByZeroError $e)
{
  echo $e->getMessage();
}
```

Before PHP 7, the preceding code would have issued a warning about the division by zero. However, now in PHP 7, it will throw a `DivisionByZeroError`, which can be handled.

New operators

PHP 7 introduced two interested operators. These operators can help write less and cleaner code, so the final code will be more readable as compared to the traditional operators in use. Let's have a look at them.

The Spaceship operator (<=>)

The Spaceship or Combined Comparison operator is useful to compare values (strings, integers, floats, and so on), arrays, and objects. This operator is just a wrapper and performs the same tasks as the three comparison operators `==`, `<`, and `>`. This operator can also be used to write clean and less code for callback functions for `usort`, `uasort`, and `uksort`. This operator works as follows:

- It returns 0 if both the operands on left- and right-hand sides are equal
- It returns -1 if the right operand is greater than the left operand
- It returns 1 if the left operand is greater than the right one

Let's take a look at a few examples by comparing integers, strings, objects, and arrays and note the result:

```
$int1 = 1;
$int2 = 2;
$int3 = 1;

echo $int1 <=> $int3; //Returns 0
echo '<br>';
echo $int1 <=> $int2; //Returns -1
echo '<br>';
echo $int2 <=> $int3; //Returns 1
```

Run the preceding code, and you will have an output similar to the following:

```
0
-1
1
```

In the first comparison, in which we compare $int1 and $int3, both are equal, so it will return 0. In the second comparison, in which $int1 and $int2 are compared, it will return -1 because the right operand ($int2) in greater than the left operand ($int1). Finally, the third comparison will return 1 as the left operand ($int2) is greater than the right operand ($int3).

The preceding is a simple example in which we compared integers. We can check strings, objects, and arrays in the same way, and they are compared the same standard PHP way.

> Some examples for the <=> operator can be found at https://wiki.php.net/rfc/combined-comparison-operator. This is an RFC publication that has more useful details about its usage.

This operator can be more useful in sorting arrays. Take a look at the following code:

```
Function normal_sort($a, $b) : int
{
  if( $a == $b )
    return 0;
  if( $a < $b )
    return -1;
  return 1;
}
```

```php
function space_sort($a, $b) : int
{
    return $a <=> $b;
}


$normalArray = [1,34,56,67,98,45];

//Sort the array in asc
usort($normalArray, 'normal_sort');

foreach($normalArray as $k => $v)
{
    echo $k.' => '.$v.'<br>';
}


$spaceArray = [1,34,56,67,98,45];

//Sort it by spaceship operator
usort($spaceArray, 'space_sort');

foreach($spaceArray as $key => $value)
{
    echo $key.' => '.$value.'<br>';
}
```

In the preceding code, we used two functions to sort the two different arrays with the same values. The $normalArray array is sorted by the normal_sort function, in which the normal_sort function uses if statements to compare the values. The second array $spaceArray has the same values as $normalArray, but this array is sorted by the space_sort function, which uses the Spaceship operator. The final result for both array sorts is the same, but the code in the callback functions is different. The normal_sort function has if statements and multiple lines of code, while the space_sort function has a single line of code—that's it! The space_sort function code is clearer and does not require multiple if statements.

The null coalesce operator(??)

We all know ternary operators, and we use them most of the time. Ternary operators are just a single-line replacement for *if-else* statements. For example, consider the following code:

```php
$post = ($_POST['title']) ? $_POST['title'] : NULL;
```

If $_POST['title'] exists, then the $post variable will be assigned its value; otherwise, NULL will be assigned. However, if $_POST or $_POST['title'] does not exist or is null, then PHP will issue a notice of *Undefined index*. To fix this notice, we need to use the isset function, as follows:

```
$post = isset($_POST['title']) ? $_POST['title'] : NULL;
```

Mostly, it will seem fine, but it becomes very nasty when we have to check for values in multiple places, especially when using PHP as a templating language.

In PHP 7, the coalescence operator is introduced, which is simple and returns the value of its first operand (left operand) if it exists and is not null. Otherwise, it returns its second operand (right operand). Consider the following example:

```
$post = $_POST['title'] ?? NULL;
```

This example is exactly similar to the preceding code. The coalesce operator checks whether $_POST['title'] exists. If it does, the operator returns it; otherwise, it returns NULL.

Another great feature of this operator is that it can be chained. Here's an example:

```
$title = $_POST['title'] ?? $_GET['title'] ?? 'No POST or GET';
```

According to the definition, it will first check whether the first operand exists and return it; if it does not exist, it will return the second operand. Now, if there is another coalesce operator used on the second operand, the same rule will be applied, and the value on the left operand will be returned if it exists. Otherwise, the value of the right operand will be returned.

So, the preceding code is the same as the following:

```
If(isset($_POST['title']))
   $title = $_POST['title'];
elseif(isset($_GET['title']))
   $title = $_GET['title'];
else
   $title = 'No POST or GET';
```

As can be noted in the preceding examples, the coalesce operator can help write clean, concise, and less code.

Uniform variable syntax

Most of the time, we may face a situation in which the method, variable, or classes
names are stored in other variables. Take a look at the following example:

```
$objects['class']->name;
```

In the preceding code, first, `$objects['class']` will be interpreted, and after this,
the property name will be interpreted. As shown in the preceding example, variables
are normally evaluated from left to right.

Now, consider the following scenario:

```
$first = ['name' => 'second'];
$second = 'Howdy';

echo $$first['name'];
```

In PHP 5.x, this code would be executed, and the output would be Howdy. However,
this is not inconsistent with the left-to-right expression evaluation. This is because
`$$first` should be evaluated first and then the index name, but in the preceding
case, it is evaluated as `${$first['name']}`. It is clear that the variable syntax is not
consistent and may create confusion. To avoid this inconsistency, PHP 7 introduced a
new syntax called uniform variable syntax. Without using this syntax, the preceding
example will bring it into notice, and the desired results won't be produced. To make
it work in PHP 7, the curly brackets should be added, as follows:

```
echo ${$first['name']};
```

Now, let's have another example, as follows:

```
class Packt
{
  public $title = 'PHP 7';
  public $publisher = 'Packt Publisher';

  public function getTitle() : string
  {
    return $this->title;
  }

  public function getPublisher() : string
  {
    return $this->publisher;
  }
}
```

```
$mthods = ['title' => 'getTitle', 'publisher' => 'getPublisher'];
$object = new Packt();
echo 'Book '.$object->$methods['title']().
  ' is published by '.$object->$methods['publisher']();
```

If the preceding code is executed in PHP 5.x, it will work fine and output our desired result. However, if we execute this code in PHP 7, it will give a fatal error. The error will be at the last line of the code, which is highlighted. PHP 7 will first try to evaluate `$object->$method`. After this, it will try to evaluate `['title']`; and so on; this is not correct.

To make it work in PHP 7, the curly brackets should be added, as in the following code:

```
echo 'Book '.$object->{$methods['title']}().
  ' is published by '.$object->{$methods['publisher']}();
```

After making the changes mentioned before, we will get our desired output.

Miscellaneous features and changes

PHP 7 also introduced some other new features with small changes, such as new syntax for array constants, multiple default cases in `switch` statement, options array in `session_start`, and so on. Let's have a look at these too.

Constant arrays

Starting with PHP 5.6, constant arrays can be initialized using the `const` keyword, as follows:

```
const STORES = ['en', 'fr', 'ar'];
```

Now, starting with PHP 7, constant arrays can be initialized using the `define` function, as follows:

```
define('STORES', ['en', 'fr', 'ar']);
```

Multiple default cases in the switch statement

Prior to PHP 7, multiple default cases in a switch statement were allowed. Check out the following example:

```
switch(true)
{
  default:
    echo 'I am first one';
```

```
      break;
   default:
     echo 'I am second one';
}
```

Before PHP 7, the preceding code was allowed, but in PHP 7, this will result in a fatal error similar to the following:

```
Fatal error: Switch statements may only contain one default clause in…
```

The options array for session_start function

Before PHP 7, whenever we needed to start a session, we just used the session_ start() function. This function did not take any arguments, and all the settings defined in php.ini were used. Now, starting with PHP 7, an optional array for options can be passed, which will override the session settings in the php.ini file.

A simple example is as follows:

```
session_start([
   'cookie_lifetime' => 3600,
   'read_and_close'  => true
]);
```

As can be seen in the preceding example, it is possible to override the php.ini settings for a session easily.

Filtered unserialize function

It is common practice to serialize and unserialize objects. However, the PHP unserialize() function was not secure because it did not have any filtering options and could unserialize objects of any type. PHP 7 introduced filtering in this function. The default filtering option is to unserialize objects of all classes or types. Its basic working is as follows:

```
$result = unserialize($object,
   ['allowed_classes' => ['Packt', 'Books', 'Ebooks']]);
```

Summary

In this chapter, we discussed new OOP features, such as type hints, anonymous classes, the throwable interface, group use declaration for namespaces, and two important new operators, the Spaceship or Combined Comparison operator and the null Coalesce operator. Also, we discussed the uniform variable syntax and a few other new features, such as new syntax for the contact array definition, options array for the `session_start()` function, and removal of multiple default cases in the switch statement.

In the next chapter, we will discuss how to improve the application's performance. We will discuss Apache and NGINX and different settings for them to improve performance.

We will discuss different settings for PHP to improve its performance. The Google page speed module, CSS/JavaScript combining and compression, CDN, and so on will also be discussed.

3
Improving PHP 7 Application Performance

PHP 7 has been completely rewritten from the ground up based on the **PHP Next Generation** (**phpng** or **PHPNG**) targeting performance. However, there are always more ways to improve the performance of the application, including writing high performance code, using best practices, web server optimizations, caching, and so on. In this chapter, we will discuss such optimizations listed as follows:

- NGINX and Apache
- HTTP server optimization
- Content Delivery Network (CDN)
- JavaScript/CSS optimization
- Full page caching
- Varnish
- The infrastructure

NGINX and Apache

There are too many HTTP server software available, and each one has its pros and cons. The two most popular HTTP servers used are NGINX and Apache. Let's have a look at both of them and note which one is better for our needs.

Apache

Apache is the most widely used HTTP server and is loved by most administrators. It is selected by administrators because of its flexibility, widespread support, power, and modules for most of the interpreted languages, such as PHP. As Apache can process a vast number of interpreted languages, it does not need to communicate with other software to fulfill the request. Apache can process requests in prefork (the processes are spawned across thread), worker (threads are spawned across processes), and event-driven (same as worker process, but it sets dedicated threads for *keep-alive* connections and separate threads for active connections); thus, it provides much more flexibility.

As discussed earlier, each request will be processed by a single thread or process, so Apache consumes too many resources. When it comes to high-traffic applications, Apache may slow down the application as it does not provide good support for concurrent processing.

NGINX

NGINX was built to solve the concurrency problems with high-traffic applications. NGINX provides asynchronous, event-driven, and nonblocking request handling. As requests are processed asynchronously, NGINX does not wait for a request to be completed to block the resource.

NGINX creates worker processes, and each individual worker process can handle thousands of connections. So, a few processes can handle high traffic at once.

NGINX does not provide any built-in support for any interpreted languages. It relies on external resources for this. This is also good because the processing is made outside NGINX, and NGINX only processes the connections and requests. Mostly, NGINX is considered faster than Apache. In some situations, such as with static content (serving images, .css and .js files, and so on), this can be true, but in current high performance servers, Apache is not the problem; PHP is the bottleneck.

 Both Apache and NGINX are available for all kinds of operations systems. For the purpose of this book, we will use Debian and Ubuntu, so all file paths will be mentioned according to these OSes

As mentioned before, we will use NGINX for this book.

HTTP server optimization

Each HTTP server provides certain features that can be used to optimize request handling and serving content. In this section, we will share some techniques for both Apache and NGINX that can be used to optimize the web server and provide the best performance and scalability. Mostly, when these optimizations are applied, a restart for Apache or NGINX is required.

Caching static files

Mostly, static files, such as images, `.css`, `.js`, and fonts don't change frequently. So, it is best practice to cache these static files on the end user machine. For this purpose, the web server adds special headers to the response, which tells the user browser to cache the static content for a certain amount of time. The following is the configuration code for both Apache and NGINX.

Apache

Let's have a look at the Apache configuration to cache the following static content:

```
<FilesMatch "\.(ico|jpg|jpeg|png|gif|css|js|woff)$">
  Header set Cache-Control "max-age=604800, public
</FileMatch>
```

In the preceding code that has to be placed in a `.htaccess` file, we used the Apache `FilesMatch` directive to match the extensions of files. If a desired extension file is requested, Apache sets the headers to cache control for seven days. The browser then caches these static files for seven days.

NGINX

The following configuration can be placed in `/etc/nginx/sites-available/your-virtual-host-conf-file`:

```
Location ~* .(ico|jpg|jpeg|png|gif|css|js|woff)$ {
  Expires 7d;
}
```

In the preceding code, we used the NGINX `Location` block with a case-insensitive modifier (`~*`) to set `Expires` for seven days. This code will set the cache-control header for seven days for all the defined file types.

After making these settings, the response headers for a request will be as follows:

```
Request Method: GET
Status Code: ● 200 OK (from cache)
▼ Response Headers
  access-control-allow-origin: *
  cache-control: max-age=604800
  content-encoding: gzip
  content-type: application/x-javascript
  date: Tue, 27 Oct 2015 11:12:10 GMT
  etag: W/"55d2213a-16d1c"
  expires: Tue, 03 Nov 2015 11:12:10 GMT
  last-modified: Mon, 17 Aug 2015 18:00:26 GMT
```

In the preceding figure, it can be clearly seen that the `.js` file is loaded from cache. Its cache-control header is set to seven days or 604,800 seconds. The expiry date can also be noted clearly in the `expires` headers. After the expiry date, the browser will load this `.js` file from the server and cache it again for the duration defined in the cache-control headers.

HTTP persistent connection

In HTTP persistent connection, or HTTP keep-alive, a single TCP/IP connection is used for multiple requests or responses. It has a huge performance improvement over the normal connection as it uses only a single connection instead of opening and closing connections for each and every single request or response. Some of the benefits of the HTTP keep-alive are as follows:

- The load on the CPU and memory is reduced because fewer TCP connections are opened at a time, and no new connections are opened for subsequent requests and responses as these TCP connections are used for them.

- Reduces latency in subsequent requests after the TCP connection is established. When a TCP connection is to be established, a three-way handshake communication is made between a user and the HTTP server. After successfully handshaking, a TCP connection is established. In case of keep-alive, the handshaking is performed only once for the initial request to establish a TCP connection, and no handshaking or TCP connection opening/closing is performed for the subsequent requests. This improves the performance of the requests/responses.

- Network congestion is reduced because only a few TCP connections are opened to the server at a time.

Besides these benefits, there are some side effects of keep-alive. Every server has a concurrency limit, and when this concurrency limit is reached or consumed, there can be a huge degradation in the application's performance. To overcome this issue, a time-out is defined for each connection, after which the HTTP keep-alive connection is closed automatically. Now, let's enable HTTP keep-alive on both Apache and NGINX.

Apache

In Apache, keep-alive can be enabled in two ways. You can enable it either in the `.htaccess` file or in the Apache config file.

To enable it in the `.htaccess` file, place the following configuration in the `.htaccess` file:

```
<ifModule mod_headers.c>
  Header set Connection keep-alive
</ifModule>
```

In the preceding configuration, we set the Connection header to keep-alive in the `.htaccess` file. As the `.htaccess` configuration overrides the configuration in the config files, this will override whatever configuration is made for keep-alive in the Apache config file.

To enable the keep-alive connection in the Apache config file, we have to modify three configuration options. Search for the following configuration and set the values to the ones in the example:

```
KeepAlive On
MaxKeepAliveRequests 100
KeepAliveTimeout 100
```

In the preceding configuration, we turned on the keep-alive configuration by setting the value of `KeepAlive` to `On`.

The next is `MaxKeepAliveRequests`, which defines the maximum number of keep-alive connections to the web server at the time. A value of 100 is the default in Apache, and it can be changed according to the requirements. For high performance, this value should be kept high. If set to 0, it will allow unlimited keep-alive connections, which is not recommended.

The last configuration is `KeepAliveTimeout`, which is set to 100 seconds. This defines the number of seconds to wait for the next request from the same client on the same TCP connection. If no request is made, then the connection is closed.

NGINX

HTTP keep-alive is part of the `http_core` module and is enabled by default. In the NGINX configuration file, we can edit a few options, such as timeout. Open the `nginx` config file, edit the following configuration options, and set its values to the following:

```
keepalive_requests 100
keepalive_timeout 100
```

The `keepalive_requests` config defines the maximum number of requests a single client can make on a single HTTP keep-alive connection.

The `keepalive_timeout` config is the number of seconds that the server needs to wait for the next request until it closes the keep-alive connection.

GZIP compression

Content compression provides a way to reduce the contents' size delivered by the HTTP server. Both Apache and NGINX provide support for GZIP compression, and similarly, most modern browsers support GZIP. When the GZIP compression is enabled, the HTTP server sends compressed HTML, CSS, JavaScript, and images that are small in size. This way, the contents are loaded fast.

A web server only compresses content via GZIP when the browser sends information about itself that it supports GZIP compression. Usually, a browser sends such information in *Request* headers.

The following are codes for both Apache and NGINX to enable GZIP compression.

Apache

The following code can be placed in the `.htaccess` file:

```
<IfModule mod_deflate.c>
SetOutputFilter DEFLATE
 #Add filters to different content types
AddOutputFilterByType DEFLATE text/html text/plain text/xml    text/
css text/javascript application/javascript
    #Don't compress images
    SetEnvIfNoCase Request_URI \.(?:gif|jpe?g|png)$ no-gzip dont-
    vary
</IfModule>
```

In the preceding code, we used the Apache `deflate` module to enable compression. We used filter by type to compress only certain types of files, such as `.html`, plain text, `.xml`, `.css`, and `.js`. Also, before ending the module, we set a case to not compress the images because compressing images can cause image quality degradation.

NGINX

As mentioned previously, you have to place the following code in your virtual host conf file for NGINX:

```
gzip on;
gzip_vary on;
gzip_types text/plain text/xml text/css text/javascript application/x-javascript;
gzip_com_level 4;
```

In the preceding code, GZIP compression is activated by the `gzip on;` line. The `gzip_vary on;` line is used to enable varying headers. The `gzip_types` line is used to define the types of files to be compressed. Any file types can be added depending on the requirements. The `gzip_com_level 4;` line is used to set the compression level, but be careful with this value; you don't want to set it too high. Its range is from 1 to 9, so keep it in the middle.

Now, let's check whether the compression really works. In the following screenshot, the request is sent to a server that does not have GZIP compression enabled. The size of the final HTML page downloaded or transferred is 59 KB:

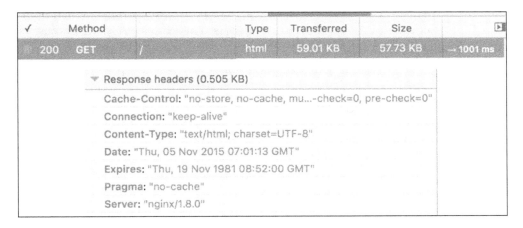

After enabling GZIP compression on the web server, the size of the transferred HTML page is reduced up to 9.95 KB, as shown in the following screenshot:

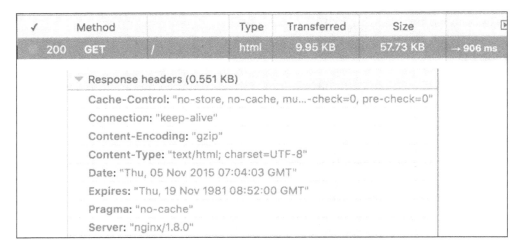

✓	Method			Type	Transferred	Size	
200	GET	/		html	9.95 KB	57.73 KB	→ 906 ms

> Response headers (0.551 KB)

Cache-Control: "no-store, no-cache, mu...-check=0, pre-check=0"

Connection: "keep-alive"

Content-Encoding: "gzip"

Content-Type: "text/html; charset=UTF-8"

Date: "Thu, 05 Nov 2015 07:04:03 GMT"

Expires: "Thu, 19 Nov 1981 08:52:00 GMT"

Pragma: "no-cache"

Server: "nginx/1.8.0"

Also, it can be noted that the time to load the contents is also reduced. So, the smaller the size of your contents, the faster the page will load.

Using PHP as a separate service

Apache uses the `mod_php` module for PHP. This way, the PHP interpreter is integrated to Apache, and all processing is done by this Apache module, which eats up more server hardware resources. It is possible to use PHP-FPM with Apache, which uses the FastCGI protocol and runs in a separate process. This enables Apache to worry about HTTP request handlings, and the PHP processing is made by the PHP-FPM.

NGINX, on the other hand, does not provide any built-in support or any support by module for PHP processing. So, with NGINX, PHP is always used in a separate service.

Now, let's take a look at what happens when PHP runs as a separate service: the web server does not know how to process the dynamic content request and forwards the request to another external service, which reduces the processing load on the web server.

Disabling unused modules

Both Apache and NGINX come with lots of modules built into them. In most cases, you won't need some of these modules. It is good practice to disable these modules.

It is good practice to make a list of the modules that are enabled, disable those modules one by one, and restart the server. After this, check whether your application is working or not. If it works, go ahead; otherwise, enable the module(s) after which the application stopped working properly again.

This is because you may see that a certain module may not be required, but some other useful module depends on this module. So, it's best practice it to make a list and enable or disable the modules, as stated before.

Apache

To list all the modules that are loaded for Apache, issue the following command in the terminal:

```
sudo apachectl -M
```

This command will list all the loaded modules, as can be seen in the following screenshot:

```
~ » apachectl -M | sort
access_compat_module (shared)
alias_module (shared)
auth_basic_module (shared)
authn_core_module (shared)
authn_file_module (shared)
authz_core_module (shared)
authz_groupfile_module (shared)
authz_host_module (shared)
authz_user_module (shared)
autoindex_module (shared)
core_module (static)
dir_module (shared)
env_module (shared)
filter_module (shared)
headers_module (shared)
hfs_apple_module (shared)
http_module (static)
lbmethod_bybusyness_module (shared)
```

Now, analyze all the loaded modules, check whether they are needed for the application, and disable them, as follows.

Open up the Apache config file and find the section where all the modules are loaded. A sample is included here:

```
LoadModule access_compat_module modules/mod_access_compat.so
LoadModule actions_module modules/mod_actions.so
LoadModule alias_module modules/mod_alias.so
LoadModule allowmethods_module modules/mod_allowmethods.so
LoadModule asis_module modules/mod_asis.so
LoadModule auth_basic_module modules/mod_auth_basic.so
#LoadModule auth_digest_module modules/mod_auth_digest.so
#LoadModule auth_form_module modules/mod_auth_form.so
#LoadModule authn_anon_module modules/mod_authn_anon.so
```

The modules that have a # sign in front of them are not loaded. So, to disable a module in the complete list, just place a # sign. The # sign will comment out the line, and the module won't be loaded anymore.

NGINX

To check which modules NGINX is compiled with, issue the following command in the terminal:

```
sudo Nginx -V
```

This will list complete information about the NGINX installation, including the version and modules with which NGINX is compiled. Have a look at the following screenshot:

```
~ # nginx -V                                                                                          root@dev
nginx version: nginx/1.8.1
built with OpenSSL 1.0.1e 11 Feb 2013
TLS SNI support enabled
configure arguments: --with-cc-opt='-g -O2 -fstack-protector --param=ssp-buffer-size=4 -Wformat -Werror=format-security
-D_FORTIFY_SOURCE=2' --with-ld-opt=-Wl,-z,relro --prefix=/usr/share/nginx --conf-path=/etc/nginx/nginx.conf --http-log-p
ath=/var/log/nginx/access.log --error-log-path=/var/log/nginx/error.log --lock-path=/var/lock/nginx.lock --pid-path=/run
/nginx.pid --http-client-body-temp-path=/var/lib/nginx/body --http-fastcgi-temp-path=/var/lib/nginx/fastcgi --http-proxy
-temp-path=/var/lib/nginx/proxy --http-scgi-temp-path=/var/lib/nginx/scgi --http-uwsgi-temp-path=/var/lib/nginx/uwsgi --
with-debug --with-pcre-jit --with-ipv6 --with-http_ssl_module --with-http_stub_status_module --with-http_realip_module -
-with-http_auth_request_module --with-http_gunzip_module --with-file-aio --with-threads --with-http_spdy_module --with-h
ttp_addition_module --with-http_dav_module --with-http_geoip_module --with-http_gzip_static_module --with-http_image_fil
ter_module --with-http_secure_link_module --with-http_sub_module --with-http_xslt_module --with-mail --with-mail_ssl_mod
ule --add-module=/usr/src/builddir/debian/modules/nginx-auth-pam --add-module=/usr/src/builddir/debian/modules/nginx-dav
-ext-module --add-module=/usr/src/builddir/debian/modules/nginx-echo --add-module=/usr/src/builddir/debian/modules/nginx
-upstream-fair --add-module=/usr/src/builddir/debian/modules/ngx_http_substitutions_filter_module --add-module=/usr/src/
builddir/debian/modules/nginx-cache-purge --add-module=/usr/src/builddir/debian/modules/ngx_http_pinba_module --add-modu
le=/usr/src/builddir/debian/modules/nginx-x-rid-header --with-ld-opt=-lossp-uuid
```

Normally, NGINX enables only those modules that are required for NGINX to work. To enable any other module that is compiled with NGINX installed, we can place a little configuration for it in the `nginx.conf` file, but there is no single way to disable any NGINX module. So, it is good to search for this specific module and take a look at the module page on the NGINX website. There, we can find information about this specific module, and if available, we can find information about how to disable and configure this module.

Web server resources

Each web server comes with its own optimum settings for general use. However, these settings may be not optimum for your current server hardware. The biggest problem on the web server hardware is the RAM. The more RAM the server has, the more the web server will be able to handle requests.

NGINX

NGINX provides two variables to adjust the resources, which are `worker_processes` and `worker_connections`. The `worker_processes` settings decide how many NGINX processes should run.

Now, how many `worker_processes` resources should we use? This depends on the server. Usually, it is one worker processes per processor core. So, if your server processor has four cores, this value can be set to 4.

The value of `worker_connections` shows the number of connections per `worker_processes` setting per second. Simply speaking, `worker_connections` tells NGINX how many simultaneous requests can be handled by NGINX. The value of `worker_connections` depends on the system processor core. To find out the core's limitations on a Linux system (Debian/Ubuntu), issue the following command in the terminal:

```
Ulimit -n
```

This command will show you a number that should be used for `worker_connections`.

Now, let's say that our processor has four cores, and each core's limitation is 512. Then, we can set the values for these two variables in the NGINX main configuration file. On Debian/Ubuntu, it is located at `/etc/nginx/nginx.conf`.

Now, find out these two variables and set them as follows:

```
Worker_processes 4;
Worker_connections 512
```

The preceding values can be high, specially `worker_connections`, because server processor cores have high limitations.

Content Delivery Network (CDN)

Content Delivery Network is used to host static media files, such as images, `.css` and `.js` files, and audio and video files. These files are stored on a geographical network whose servers are located in different locations. Then, these files are served to requests from a specific server, depending on the request location.

CDN provides the following features:

- As the contents are static, which don't change frequently, CDN caches them in memory. When a request comes for a certain file, CDN sends the file directly from cache, which is faster than loading the file from disk and sending it to the browser.

- CDN servers are located in different locations. All the files are stored in each location, depending on your settings in CDN. When a browser request arrives to CDN, CDN sends the requested contents from the nearest location available to the requested location. For example, if the CDN has servers in London, New York, and Dubai and a request comes from Middle East, the CDN will send content from the Dubai server. This way, as a CDN delivers the contents from the nearest location, the response time is reduced.

- Each browser has limitations for sending simultaneous requests to a domain. Mostly, it's three requests. When a response arrives for a request, the browser sends more requests to the same domain, which causes a delay in complete page loading. CDN provides subdomains (either their own subdomains or your main domain's subdomains, using your main domain's DNS settings), which enables browsers to send more parallel requests for the same contents loading from different domains. This enables the browser to load the page content fast.

- Generally, there is a small amount of requests for dynamic content and more requests for static content. If your application's static content is hosted on a separate CDN server, this will reduce the load on your server tremendously.

Using CDN

So, how do you use CDN in your application? In best practice, if your application has high traffic, creating different subdomains at your CDN for each content type is the best. For example, a separate domain for CSS and JavaScript files, a subdomain for images, and another separate subdomain for audio/videos files can be created. This way, the browser will send parallel requests for each content type. Let's say, we have the following URLs for each content type:

- **For CSS and JavaScript**: `http://css-js.yourcdn.com`

- **For images**: `http://images.yourcdn.com`
- **For other media**: `http://media.yourcdn.com`

Now, most open source applications provide settings at their admin control panel to set up CDN URLs, but in case you happened to use an open source framework or a custom-build application, you can define your own setting for CDN by placing the previous URLs either in the database or in a configuration file loaded globally.

For our example, we will place the preceding URLs in a config file and create three constants for them, as follows:

```
Constant('CSS_JS_URL', 'http://css-js.yourcdn.com/');
Constant('IMAGES_URL', 'http://images.yourcdn.com/');
Constant('MEDiA_URL', 'http://css-js.yourcdn.com/');
```

If we need to load a CSS file, it can be loaded as follows:

```
<script type="text/javascript" src="<?php echo CSS_JS_URL
?>js/file.js"></script>
```

For a JavaScript file, it can be loaded as follows:

```
<link rel="stylesheet" type="text/css" href="<?php echo CSS_JS_URL
?>css/file.css" />
```

If we load images, we can use the previous way in the `src` attribute of the `img` tag, as follows:

```
<img src="<?php echo IMAGES_URL ?>images/image.png" />
```

In the preceding examples, if we don't need to use CDN or want to change the CDN URLs, it will be easy to change in just one place.

Most famous JavaScript libraries and templating engines host their static resources on their own personal CDN. Google hosts query libraries, fonts, and other JavaScript libraries on its own CDN, which can be used directly in applications.

Sometimes, we may not want to use CDN or be able to afford them. For this, we can use a technique called domain sharing. Using domain sharding, we can create subdomains or point out other domains to our resources' directories on the same server and application. The technique is the same as discussed earlier; the only difference is that we direct other domains or subdomains to our media, CSS, JavaScript, and image directories ourselves.

This may seem be fine, but it won't provide us with CDN's best performance. This is because CDN decides the geographical availability of content depending on the customer's location, extensive caching, and files optimization on the fly.

CSS and JavaScript optimization

Every web application has CSS and JavaScript files. Nowadays, it is common that most applications have lots of CSS and JavaScript files to make the application attractive and interactive. Each CSS and JavaScript file needs a browser to send a request to the server to fetch the file. So, the more the CSS and JavaScript files you have, the more requests the browser will need to send, thus affecting its performance.

Each file has a content size, and it takes time for the browser to download it. For example, if we have 10 CSS files of 10 KB each and 10 JavaScript files of 50 KB each, the total content size of the CSS files is 100 KB, and for JavaScript it is 500 KB – 600 KB for both types of files. This is too much, and the browser will take time to download them.

 Performance plays a vital role in web applications. Even Google counts performance in its indexing. Don't think of a file that has a few KBs and takes a 1 ms to download because when it comes to performance, each millisecond is counted. The best thing is to optimize, compress, and cache everything.

In this section, we will discuss two ways to optimize our CSS and JS, which are as follows:

- Merging
- Minifying

Merging

In the merging process, we can merge all the CSS files into a single file, and the same process is carried out with JavaScript files, thus creating a single file for CSS and JavaScript. If we have 10 files for CSS, the browser sends 10 requests for all these files. However, if we merge them in a single file, the browser will send only one request, and thus, the time taken for nine requests is saved.

Minifying

In the minifying process, all the empty lines, comments, and extra spaces are removed from the CSS and JavaScript files. This way, the size of the file is reduced, and the file loads fast.

For example, let's say you have the following CSS code in a file:

```
.header {
  width: 1000px;
```

```
    height: auto;
    padding: 10px
}

/* move container to left */
.float-left {
  float: left;
}

/* Move container to right */
.float-right {
  float: right;
}
```

After minifying the file, we will have CSS code similar to the following:

```
.header{width:100px;height:auto;padding:10px}.float-
left{float:left}.float-right{float:right}
```

Similarly for JavaScript, let's consider that we have the following code in a JavaScript file:

```
/* Alert on page load */
$(document).ready(function() {
  alert("Page is loaded");
});

/* add three numbers */
function addNumbers(a, b, c) {
  return a + b + c;
}
```

Now, if the preceding file is minified, we will have the following code:

```
$(document).ready(function(){alert("Page is loaded")});
function addNumbers(a,b,c){return a+b+c;}
```

It can be noted in the preceding examples that all the unnecessary white spaces and new lines are removed. Also, it places the complete file code in one single line. All code comments are removed. This way, the file size is reduced, which helps the file be loaded fast. Also, this file will consume less bandwidth, which is useful if the server resources are limited.

Most open source applications, such as Magento, Drupal, and WordPress, provide either built-in support or support the application by third-party plugins/modules. Here, we won't cover how to merge CSS or JavaScript files in these applications, but we will discuss a few tools that can merge CSS and JavaScript files.

Minify

Minify is a set of libraries completely written in PHP. Minify supports both merging and minifying for both CSS and JavaScript files. Its code is completely object-oriented and namespaced, so it can be embedded into any current or proprietary framework.

 The Minify homepage is located at `http://minifier.org`. It is also hosted on GitHub at `https://github.com/matthiasmullie/minify`. It is important to note that the Minify library uses a path converter library, which is written by the same author. The path converter library can be downloaded from `https://github.com/matthiasmullie/path-converter`. Download this library and place it in the same folder as the minify libraries.

Now, let's create a small project that we will use to minify and merge CSS and JavaScript files. The folder structure of the project will be as in the following screenshot:

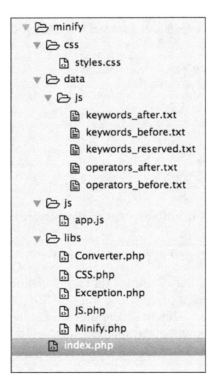

In the preceding screenshot, the complete project structure is shown. The project name is `minify`. The `css` folder has all of our CSS files, including the minified or merged ones. Similarly, the `js` folder has all our JavaScript files, including the minified or merged ones. The `libs` folder has the `Minify` library along with the `Converter` library. `Index.php` has our main code to minify and merge CSS and JavaScript files.

> The `data` folder in the project tree is related to JavaScript minification. As JavaScript has keywords that require a space before and after them, these `.txt` files are used to identify these operators.

So, let's start by minifying our CSS and JavaScript files using the following code in `index.php`:

```
include('libs/Converter.php');
include('libs/Minify.php');
include('libs/CSS.php');
include('libs/JS.php');
include('libs/Exception.php');

use MatthiasMullie\Minify;

/* Minify CSS */
$cssSourcePath = 'css/styles.css';
$cssOutputPath = 'css/styles.min.css';
$cssMinifier = new Minify\CSS($cssSourcePath);
$cssMinifier->minify($cssOutputPath);

/* Minify JS */
$jsSourcePath = 'js/app.js';
$jsOutputPath = 'js/app.min.js';
$jsMinifier = new Minify\JS($jsSourcePath);
$jsMinifier->minify($jsOutputPath);
```

The preceding code is simple. First, we included all our required libraries. Then, in the `Minify CSS` block, we created two path variables: `$cssSourcePath`, which has the path to the CSS file that we need to minify, and `$cssOutputPath`, which has path to the minified CSS file that will be generated.

After this, we instantiated an object of the `CSS.php` class and passed the CSS file that we need to minify. Finally, we called the minify method of the `CSS` class and passed the output path along with the filename, which will generate the required file for us.

The same explanation goes for the JS minifying process.

If we run the preceding PHP code, all the files are in place, and everything goes fine, then two new filenames will be created: `styles.min.css` and `app.min.js`. These are the new minified versions of their original files.

Now, let's use Minify to merge multiple CSS and JavaScript files. First, add some CSS and JavaScript files to the respective folders in the project. After this, we just need to add a little code to the current code. In the following code, I will skip including all the libraries, but these files have to be loaded whenever you need to use Minify:

```
/* Minify CSS */
$cssSourcePath = 'css/styles.css';
$cssOutputPath = 'css/styles.min.merged.css';
$cssMinifier = new Minify\CSS($cssSourcePath);
$cssMinifier->add('css/style.css');
$cssMinifier->add('css/forms.js');
$cssMinifier->minify($cssOutputPath);

/* Minify JS */
$jsSourcePath = 'js/app.js';
$jsOutputPath = 'js/app.min.merged.js';
$jsMinifier = new Minify\JS($jsSourcePath);
$jsMinifier->add('js/checkout.js');
$jsMinifier->minify($jsOutputPath);
```

Now, take a look at the highlighted code. In the CSS part, we saved the minified and merged file as `style.min.merged.css`, but naming is not important; it is all up to our own choice.

Now, we will simply use the add method of the `$cssMinifier` and `$jsMinifier` objects to add new files and then call `minify`. This causes all the additional files to be merged in the initial file and then minified, thus generating a single merged and minified file.

Grunt

According to its official website, Grunt is a JavaScript task runner. It automates certain repetitive tasks so that you don't have to work repeatedly. It is an awesome tool and is widely used among web programmers.

Installing Grunt is very easy. Here, we will install it on MAC OS X, and the same method is used for most Linux systems, such as Debian and Ubuntu.

Grunt requires Node.js and npm. Installing and configuring Node.js and npm is out of the scope of this book, so for this book, we will assume that these tools are installed on your machine or that you can search for them and figure out how to install them.

If Node.js and npm are installed on your machine, just fire up the following command in your terminal:

```
sudo npm install -g grunt
```

This will install Grunt CLI. If everything goes fine, then the following command will show you the version the of Grunt CLI:

```
grunt -version
```

The output of the preceding command is `grunt-cli v0.1.13`; as of writing this book, this version is available.

Grunt provides you with a command-line, which enables you to run a Grunt command. A Grunt project requires two files in your project file tree. One is `package.json`, which is used by `npm` and lists Grunt and the Grunt plugins that the project needs as DevDependencies.

The second file is the `GruntFile`, which is stored as `GruntFile.js` or `GruntFile.coffee` and is used to configure and define Grunt tasks and load Grunt plugins.

Now, we will use the same preceding project, but our folder structure will be as follows:

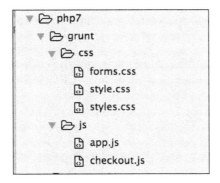

Now, open the terminal in your project root and issue the following command:

```
sudo npm init
```

This will generate the `package.json` file by asking a few questions. Now, open the `package.json` file and modify it so that the contents of the final `package.json` files look similar to the following:

```
{
   "name" : "grunt"  //Name of the project
   "version : "1.0.0" //Version of the project
   "description" : "Minify and Merge JS and CSS file",
   "main" : "index.js",
   "DevDependencies" : {
     "grunt" : "0.4.1", //Version of Grunt

     //Concat plugin version used to merge css and js files
     "grunt-contrib-concat" : "0.1.3"

     //CSS minifying plugin
     "grunt-contrib-cssmin" : "0.6.1",

     //Uglify plugin used to minify JS files.
     "grunt-contrib-uglify" : "0.2.0"

   },
  "author" : "Altaf Hussain",
  "license" : ""
  }
```

I added comments to different parts of the `package.json` file so that it is easy to understand. Note that for the final file, we will remove the comments from this file.

It can be seen that in the `DevDependencies` section, we added three Grunt plugins used for different tasks.

The next step is to add `GruntFile`. Let's create a file called `GruntFile.js` in our project root similar to the `package.json` file. Place the following contents in `GruntFile`:

```
module.exports = function(grunt) {
   /*Load the package.json file*/
   pkg: grunt.file.readJSON('package.json'),
   /*Define Tasks*/
   grunt.initConfig({
     concat: {
       css: {
         src: [
           'css/*' //Load all files in CSS folder
```

```
        ],
                dest: 'dest/combined.css' //Destination of the final combined
        file.

            }, //End of CSS
        js: {
            src: [
            'js/*' //Load all files in js folder
        ],
                dest: 'dest/combined.js' //Destination of the final combined
        file.

            }, //End of js

        }, //End of concat
        cssmin:  {
          css: {
            src : 'dest/combined.css',
            dest : 'dest/combined.min.css'
        }
        },//End of cssmin
        uglify: {
          js: {
            files: {
              'dest/combined.min.js' : ['dest/combined.js'] // destination
                Path : [src path]
            }
          }
        } //End of uglify

        }); //End of initConfig

        grunt.loadNpmTasks('grunt-contrib-concat');
        grunt.loadNpmTasks('grunt-contrib-uglify');
        grunt.loadNpmTasks('grunt-contrib-cssmin');
        grunt.registerTask('default', ['concat:css', 'concat:js',
          'cssmin:css', 'uglify:js']);

        }; //End of module.exports
```

The preceding code is simple and self-explanatory, and the comments are added whenever needed. At the top, we loaded our package.json file, and after this, we defined different tasks along with their src and destination files. Remember that every task's src and destination syntax is different, and it depends on the plugin. After initConfig block, we loaded different plugins and npm tasks and then registered them with GRUNT.

Now, let's run our tasks.

First, let's combine CSS and JavaScript files and store them in their respective destinations defined in our tasks list in GruntFile via the following command:

```
grunt concat
```

After running the preceding command in your terminal, if you see a message such as `Done, without errors`, then the task is completed successfully.

In the same way, let's minify our css file using the following command:

```
grunt cssmin
```

Then, we will minify our JavaScript file using the following command:

```
grunt uglify
```

Now, it may seem like a lot of work to use Grunt, but it provides some other features that can make a developer's life easy. For example, what if you need to change your JavaScript and CSS files? Should you run all the preceding commands again? No, Grunt provides a watch plugin, which activates and executes all the files in the destination paths in the tasks, and if any changes occur, it runs the tasks automatically.

For a more detailed learning, take a look at Grunt's official website at `http://gruntjs.com/`.

Full page caching

In full page caching, the complete page of the website is stored in a cache, and for the next requests, this cached page is served. Full page cache is more effective if your website content does not change too often; for example, on a blog with simple posts, new posts are added on a weekly basis. In this case, the cache can be cleared after new posts are added.

What if you have a website that has pages with dynamic parts, such as an e-commerce website? In this case, a complete page caching will create problems because the page is always different for each request; as a user is logged in, he/she may add products to the shopping cart and so on. In this case, using full page caching may not be that easy.

Most popular platforms provide either built-in support for full page cache or through plugins and modules. In this case, the plugin or module takes care of the dynamic blocks of the page for each request.

Varnish

Varnish, as mentioned on its official website, makes your website fly; and this is true! Varnish is an open source web application accelerator that runs in front of your web server software. It has to be configured on port 80 so that each request comes to it.

Now, the Varnish configuration file (called VCL files with the `.vcl` extenstion) has a definition for backends. A backend is the web server (Apache or NGINX) configured on another port (let's say 8080). Multiple backends can be defined, and Varnish will take care of the load balancing too.

When a request comes to Varnish, it checks whether the data for this request in available at its cache or not. If it finds the data in its cache, this cached data is returned to the request, and no request is sent to the web server or backend. If Varnish does not find any data in its cache, it sends a request to the web server and requests the data. When it receives data from the web server, it first caches this data and then sends it back to the request.

As it is clear in the preceding discussion, if Varnish finds the data in the cache, there is no need for a request to the web server and, therefore, for processing in there, and the response is sent back very fast.

Varnish also provides features such as load balancing and health checks. Also, Varnish has no support for SSL and cookies. If Varnish receives cookies from the web server or backend, this page is not cached. There are different ways to overcome these issues easily.

We've done enough theory; now, let's install Varnish on a Debian/Ubuntu server via the following steps:

1. First, add the Varnish repositories to the `sources.list` file. Place the following line in the file:

   ```
   deb https://repo.varnish-cache.org/debian/ Jessie
      varnish-4.1
   ```

2. After this, issue the following command to update the repositories:

   ```
   sudo apt-get update
   ```

3. Now, issue the following command:

   ```
   sudo apt-get install varnish
   ```

4. This will download and install Varnish. Now, the first thing to do is configure Varnish to listen at port 80 and make your web server listen at another port, such as 8080. We will configure it here with NGINX.

5. Now, open the Varnish configuration file location at `/etc/default/varnish` and change it so that it looks similar to the following code:

```
DAEMON_OPS="-a :80 \
  -T localhost:6082 \
  -f /etc/varnish/default.vcl \
  -S /etc/varnish/secret \
  -s malloc,256m"
```

6. Save the file and restart Varnish by issuing the following command in the terminal:

```
sudo service varnish restart
```

7. Now our Varnish runs on port 80. Let's make NGINX run on port 8080. Edit the NGINX `vhost` file for the application and change the listen port from 80 to 8080, as follows:

```
listen 8080;
```

8. Now, restart NGINX by issuing the following command in the terminal:

```
sudo service nginx restart
```

9. The next step is to configure the Varnish VCL file and add a backend that will communicate with our backend on port 8080. Edit the Varnish VCL file located at `/etc/varnish/default.vcl`, as follows:

```
backend default {
  .host = "127.0.0.1";
  .port = "8080";
}
```

In the preceding configuration, our backend host is located at the same server on which Varnish runs, so we entered the local IP. We can also enter a localhost in this case. However, if our backend runs on a remote host or another server, the IP of this server should be entered.

Now, we are done with Varnish and web server configuration. Restart both Varnish and NGINX. Open your browser and enter the IP or hostname of the server. The first response may seem slow, which is because Varnish is fetching data from the backend and then caching it, but other subsequent responses will be extremely fast, as Varnish cached them and is now sending back the cached data without communicating with the backend.

Varnish provides a tool in which we can easily monitor the Varnish cache status. It is a real-time tool and updates its contents in real time. It is called varnishstat. To start varnishstat, just issue the following command in the terminal:

```
varnishstat
```

The preceding command will display a session similar to the following screenshot:

NAME	CURRENT	CHANGE	AVERAGE	AVG_10	AVG_100	AVG_1000
MAIN.uptime	0+00:18:43					
MAIN.sess_conn	107	0.00	.	0.00	0.10	0.18
MAIN.client_req	1368	0.00	1.00	0.00	1.25	2.28
MAIN.cache_hit	867	0.00	.	0.00	0.81	1.68
MAIN.cache_miss	454	0.00	.	0.00	0.35	0.48
MAIN.backend_reuse	540	0.00	.	0.00	0.46	0.68
MAIN.backend_recycle	556	0.00	.	0.00	0.48	0.70
MAIN.fetch_length	381	0.00	.	0.00	0.29	0.41
MAIN.fetch_chunked	105	0.00	.	0.00	0.10	0.15
MAIN.fetch_304	70	0.00	.	0.00	0.08	0.14
MAIN.pools	2	0.00	.	2.00	2.00	2.00
MAIN.threads	200	0.00	.	200.00	200.00	200.00
MAIN.threads_created	200	0.00	.	0.00	0.00	0.00
MAIN.n_object	431	0.00	.	431.01	402.38	371.67
MAIN.n_objectcore	436	0.00	.	436.01	403.94	371.70
MAIN.n_objecthead	441	0.00	.	441.08	413.18	381.57
MAIN.n_backend	1	0.00	.	1.00	1.00	1.00
MAIN.n_expired	23	0.00	.	22.99	21.20	19.78
MAIN.s_sess	107	0.00	.	0.00	0.10	0.18
MAIN.s_req	1368	0.00	1.00	0.00	1.25	2.28
MAIN.s_pass	86	0.00	.	0.00	0.12	0.17
MAIN.s_fetch	540	0.00	.	0.00	0.47	0.65
MAIN.s_req_hdrbytes	1.54M	0.00	1.40K	0.05	1.42K	2.61K
MAIN.s_req_bodybytes	1.06K	0.00	.	0.00	1.46	1.81
MAIN.s_resp_hdrbytes	578.96K	0.00	527.00	0.02	534.70	969.56
MAIN.s_resp_bodybytes	3.15M	0.00	2.88K	0.04	1.84K	3.22K
MAIN.backend_req	556	0.00	.	0.00	0.48	0.70
hvy MAIN_uptime					INFO	1-27/48

As can be seen in the preceding screenshot, it displays very useful information, such as the running time and the number of requests made at the beginning, cache hits, cache misses, all backends, backend reusages, and so on. We can use this information to tune Varnish for its best performance.

 A complete Varnish configuration is out of the scope of this book, but a good documentation can be found on the Varnish official website at https://www.varnish-cache.org.

The infrastructure

We discussed too many topics on increasing the performance of our application. Now, let's discuss the scalability and availability of our application. With time, the traffic on our application can increase to thousands of users at a time. If our application runs on a single server, the performance will be hugely effected. Also, it is not a good idea to keep the application running at a single point because in case this server goes down, our complete application will be down.

To make our application more scalable and better in availability, we can use an infrastructure setup in which we can host our application on multiple servers. Also, we can host different parts of the application on different servers. To better understand, take a look at the following diagram:

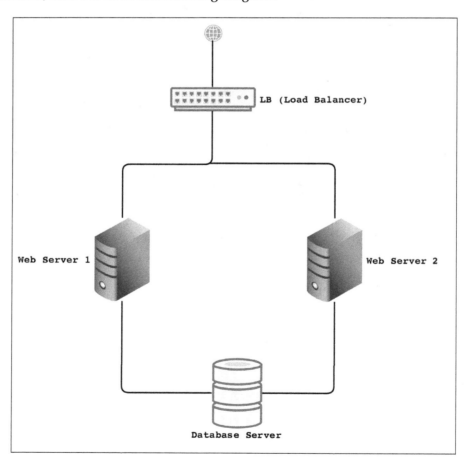

This is a very basic design for the infrastructure. Let's talk about its different parts and what operations will be performed by each part and server.

 It is possible that only the Load Balancer (LB) will be connected to the public Internet, and the rest of the parts can be connected to each through a private network in a Rack. If a Rack is available, this will be very good because all the communication between all the servers will be on a private network and therefore secure.

Web servers

In the preceding diagram, we have two web servers. There can be as many web servers as needed, and they can be easily connected to LB. The web servers will host our actual application, and the application will run on NGINX or Apache and PHP 7. All the performance tunings we will discuss in this chapter can be used on these web servers. Also, it is not necessary that these servers should be listening at port 80. It is good that our web server should listen at another port to avoid any public access using browsers.

The database server

The database server is mainly used for the database where the MySQL or Percona Server can be installed. However, one of the problems in the infrastructure setup is to store session data in a single place. For this purpose, we can also install the Redis server on the database server, which will handle our application's session data.

The preceding infrastructure design is not a final or perfect design. It is just to give the idea of a multiserver application hosting. It has room for a lot of improvement, such as adding another local balancer, more web servers, and servers for the database cluster.

Load balancer (LB)

The first part is the **load balancer** (**LB**). The purpose of the load balancer is to divide the traffic among the web servers according to the load on each web server.

For the load balancer, we can use HAProxy, which is widely used for this purpose. Also, HAProxy checks the health of each web server, and if a web server is down, it automatically redirects the traffic of this down web server to other available web servers. For this purpose, only LB will be listening at port 80.

We don't want to place a load on our available web servers (in our case, two web servers) of encrypting and decrypting the SSL communication, so we will use the HAProxy server to terminate SSL there. When our LB receives a request with SSL, it will terminate SSL and send a normal request to one of the web servers. When it receives a response, HAProxy will encrypt the response and send it back to the client. This way, instead of using both the servers for SSL encryption/decryption, only a single LB server will be used for this purpose.

 Varnish can be also used as a load balancer, but this is not a good idea because the whole purpose of Varnish is HTTP caching.

HAProxy load balancing

In the preceding infrastructure, we placed a load balancer in front of our web servers, which balance load on each server, check the health of each server, and terminate SSL. We will install HAProxy and configure it to achieve all the configurations mentioned before.

HAProxy installation

We will install HAProxy on Debian/Ubuntu. As of writing this book, HAProxy 1.6 is the latest stable version available. Perform the following steps to install HAProxy:

1. First, update the system cache by issuing the following command in the terminal:

    ```
    sudo apt-get update
    ```

2. Next, install HAProxy by entering the following command in the terminal:

    ```
    sudo apt-get install haproxy
    ```

    This will install HAProxy on the system.

3. Now, confirm the HAProxy installation by issuing the following command in the terminal:

    ```
    haproxy -v
    ```

```
~ # haproxy -v
HA-Proxy version 1.5.8 2014/10/31
Copyright 2000-2014 Willy Tarreau <w@1wt.eu>


~ #
```

If the output is as in the preceding screenshot, then congratulations! HAProxy is installed successfully.

HAProxy load balancing

Now, it's time to use HAProxy. For this purpose, we have the following three servers:

- The first is a load balancer server on which HAProxy is installed. We will call it LB. For this book's purpose, the IP of the LB server is 10.211.55.1. This server will listen at port 80, and all HTTP requests will come to this server. This server also acts as a frontend server as all the requests to our application will come to this server.

- The second is a web server, which we will call Web1. NGINX, PHP 7, MySQL, or Percona Server are installed on it. The IP of this server is 10.211.55.2. This server will either listen at port 80 or any other port. We will keep it to listen at port 8080.

- The third is a second web server, which we will call Web2, with the IP 10.211.55.3. This has the same setup as of the Web1 server and will listen at port 8080.

The Web1 and Web2 servers are also called backend servers. First, let's configure the LB or frontend server to listen at port 80.

Open the `haproxy.cfg` file located at `/etc/haproxy/` and add the following lines at the end of the file:

```
frontend http
   bind *:80
   mode http
   default_backend web-backends
```

In the preceding code, we set HAProxy to listen at the HTTP port 80 on any IP address, either the local loopback IP 127.0.0.1 or the public IP. Then, we set the default backend.

Now, we will add two backend servers. In the same file, at the end, place the following code:

```
backend web-backend
    mode http
    balance roundrobin
    option forwardfor
    server web1 10.211.55.2:8080 check
    server web2 10.211.55.3:8080 check
```

In the preceding configuration, we added two servers into the web backend. The reference name for the backend is `web-backend`, which is used in the frontend configuration too. As we know, both our web servers listen at port 8080, so we mentioned that it is the definition of each web server. Also, we used `check` at the end of the definition of each web server, which tells HAProxy to check the server's health.

Now, restart HAProxy by issuing the following command in the terminal:

`sudo service haproxy restart`

> To start HAProxy, we can use the `sudo service haproxy start` command. To stop HAProxy, we can use the `sudo service haproxy stop` command.

Now, enter the IP or hostname of the LB server in the browser, and our web application page will be displayed either from Web1 or Web2.

Now, disable any of the web servers and then reload the page again. The application will still work fine, because HAProxy automatically detected that one of web servers is down and redirected the traffic to the second web server.

HAProxy also provides a stats page, which is browser-based. It provides complete monitoring information about the LB and all the backends. To enable stats, open `haprox.cfg`, and place the following code at the end of the file:

```
listen stats *:1434
    stats enable
    stats uri /haproxy-stats
    stats auth phpuser:packtPassword
```

The stats are enabled at port `1434`, which can be set to any port. The URL of the page is `stats uri`. It can be set to any URL. The `auth` section is for basic HTTP authentication. Save the file and restart HAProxy. Now, open the browser and enter the URL, such as `10.211.55.1:1434/haproxy-stats`. The stats page will be displayed as follows:

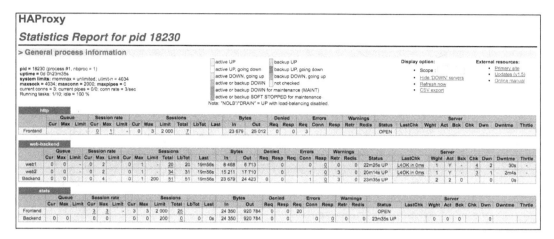

In the preceding screenshot, each backend web server can be seen, including frontend information.

Also, if a web server is down, HAProxy stats will highlight the row for this web server, as can be seen in the following screenshot:

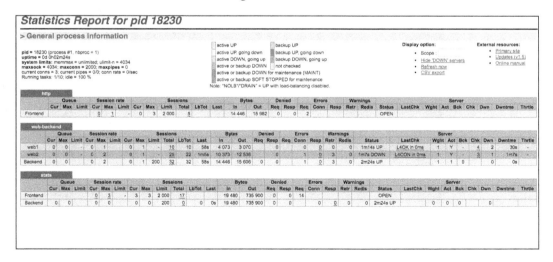

For our test, we stopped NGINX at our Web2 server and refreshed the stats page, and the Web2 server row in the backend section was highlighted.

To terminate SSL using HAProxy, it is pretty simple. To terminate SSL using HAProxy, we will just add the SSL port 443 binding along with the SSL certificate file location. Open the `haproxy.cfg` file, edit the frontend block, and add the highlighted code in it, as in the following block:

```
frontend http
bind *:80
bind *:443 ssl crt /etc/ssl/www.domain.crt
  mode http
  default_backend web-backends
```

Now, HAProxy also listens at 443, and when an SSL request is sent to it, it processes it there and terminates it so that no HTTPS requests are sent to backend servers. This way, the load of SSL encryption/decryption is removed from the web servers and is managed by the HAProxy server only. As SSL is terminated at the HAProxy server, there is no need for web servers to listen at port 443, as regular requests from HAProxy server are sent to the backend.

Summary

In this chapter, we discussed several topics starting from NGINX and Apache to Varnish. We discussed how we can optimize our web server's software settings for the best performance. Also, we discussed CDNs and how to use them in our customer applications. We discussed two ways to optimize JavaScript and CSS files for the best performance. We briefly discussed full page cache and Varnish installation and configuration. At the end, we discussed multiserver hosting or infrastructure setup for our application to be scalable and the best in availability.

In next chapter, we will look into the ways of increasing the performance of our database. We will discuss several topics, including the Percona Server, different storage engines for the database, query caching, Redis, and Memcached.

4
Improving Database Performance

Databases play a key role in dynamic websites. All incoming and outgoing data is stored in a database. So, if the database for a PHP application is not well designed and optimized, it will effect the application's performance tremendously. In this chapter, we will look into the ways of optimizing our PHP application's database. The following topics will be covered in this chapter:

- MySQL
- Query caching
- The MyISAM and InnoDB storage engines
- The Percona DB and Percona XtraDB storage engines
- MySQL performance monitoring tools
- Redis
- Memcached

The MySQL database

MySQL is the most commonly used **Relational Database Management System (RDMS)** for the Web. It is open source and has a free community version. It provides all those features that can be provided by an enterprise-level database.

The default settings provided with the MySQL installation may not be so good for performance, and there are always ways to fine-tune these settings to get an improved performance. Also, remember that your database design plays a big role in performance. A poorly designed database will have an effect on the overall performance.

In this section, we will discuss how to improve the MySQL database's performance.

 We will modify the MySQL configuration's `my.cnf` file. This file is located in different places in different operating systems. Also, if you are using XAMPP, WAMP, or any other cross-platform web server solution stack package on Windows, this file will be located in the respective folder. Whenever `my.cnf` is mentioned, it is assumed that the file is open no matter which OS is used.

Query caching

Query caching is an important performance feature of MySQL. It caches SELECT queries along with the resulting dataset. When an identical SELECT query occurs, MySQL fetches the data from memory so that the query is executed faster and thus reduces the load on the database.

To check whether query cache is enabled on a MySQL server or not, issue the following command in your MySQL command line:

```
SHOW VARIABLES LIKE 'have_query_cache';
```

The preceding command will display the following output:

```
mysql> SHOW VARIABLES LIKE 'have_query_cache';
+------------------+-------+
| Variable_name    | Value |
+------------------+-------+
| have_query_cache | YES   |
+------------------+-------+
1 row in set (0.00 sec)

mysql> _
```

The previous result set shows that query cache is enabled. If query cache is disabled, the value will be NO.

To enable query caching, open up the `my.cnf` file and add the following lines. If these lines are there and are commented, just uncomment them:

```
query_cache_type = 1
query_cache_size = 128MB
query_cache_limit = 1MB
```

Save the `my.cnf` file and restart the MySQL server. Let's discuss what the preceding three configurations mean:

- `query_cache_type`: This plays a little confusing role.

  - If `query_cache_type` is set to `1` and `query_cache_size` is 0, then no memory is allocated, and query cache is disabled.

    If `query_cache_size` is greater than 0, then query cache is enabled, memory is allocated, and all queries that do not exceed the `query_cache_limit` value or use the `SQL_NO_CACHE` option are cached.

  - If the `query_cache_type` value is 0 and `query_cache_size` is 0, then no memory is allocated, and cache is disabled.

    If `query_cache_size` is greater than 0, then memory is allocated, but nothing is cached — that is, cache is disabled.

- `query_cache_size`: `query_cache_size`: This indicates how much memory will be allocated. Some think that the more memory is used, the better it will be, but this is just a misunderstanding. It all depends on the database size, query types and ratios between read and writes, hardware, database traffic, and other factors. A good value for `query_cache_size` is between 100 MB and 200 MB; then, you can monitor the performance and other variables on which query cache depends, as mentioned, and adjust the size. We have used 128MB for a medium traffic Magento website and it is working perfectly. Set this value to `0` to disable query cache.

- `query_cache_limit`: This defines the maximum size of a query dataset to be cached. If a query dataset's size is larger than this value, it isn't cached. The value of this configuration can be guessed by finding out the largest `SELECT` query and the size of its returned dataset.

Storage engines

Storage engines (or table types) are a part of core MySQL and are responsible for handling operations on tables. MySQL provides several storage engines, and the two most widely used are MyISAM and InnoDB. Both these storage engines have their own pros and cons, but InnoDB is always prioritized. MySQL started using InnoDB as the default storage engine, starting from 5.5.

MySQL provides some other storage engines that have their own purposes. During the database design process, which table should use which storage engine can be decided. A complete list of storage engines for MySQL 5.6 can be found at `http://dev.mysql.com/doc/refman/5.6/en/storage-engines.html`.

A storage engine can be set at database level, which is then used as the default storage engine for each newly created table. Note that the storage engine is the table's base, and different tables can have different storage engines in a single database. What if we have a table already created and want to change its storage engine? It is easy. Let's say that our table name is `pkt_users`, its storage engine is MyISAM, and we want to change it to InnoDB; we will use the following MySQL command:

```
ALTER TABLE pkt_users ENGINE=INNODB;
```

This will change the storage engine value of the table to `INNODB`.

Now, let's discuss the difference between the two most widely used storage engines: MyISAM and InnoDB.

The MyISAM storage engine

A brief list of features that are or are not supported by MyISAM is as follows:

- MyISAM is designed for speed, which plays best with the `SELECT` statement.
- If a table is more static—that is, the data in this table is less frequently updated/deleted and mostly only fetched—then MyISAM is the best option for this table.
- MyISAM supports table-level locking. If a specific operation needs to be performed on the data in a table, then the complete table can be locked. During this lock, no operations can be performed on this table. This can cause performance degradation if the table is more dynamic—that is, if the data is frequently changed in this table.
- MyISAM does not have support for foreign keys.
- MyISAM supports full-text search.
- MyISAM does not support transactions. So, there is no support for `COMMIT` and `ROLLBACK`. If a query on a table is executed, it is executed, and there is no coming back.
- Data compression, replication, query caching, and data encryption is supported.
- The cluster database is not supported.

The InnoDB storage engine

A brief list of features that are or are not supported by InnoDB is as follows:

- InnoDB is designed for high reliability and high performance when processing a high volume of data.

- InnoDB supports row-level locking. It is a good feature and is great for performance. Instead of locking the complete table as with MyISAM, it locks only the specific row for the SELECT, DELETE, or UPDATE operations, and during these operations, other data in this table can be manipulated.

- InnoDB supports foreign keys and forcing foreign keys constraints.

- Transactions are supported. COMMIT and ROLLBACK are possible, so data can be recovered from a specific transaction.

- Data compression, replication, query caching, and data encryption is supported.

- InnoDB can be used in a cluster environment, but it does not have full support. However, InnoDB tables can be converted to the NDB storage engine, which is used in the MySQL cluster by changing the table engine to NDB.

In the following sections, we will discuss some more performance features that are related to InnoDB. Values for the following configuration are set in the my.cnf file.

innodb_buffer_pool_size

This setting defines how much memory should be used for InnoDB data and the indices loaded into memory. For a dedicated MySQL server, the recommended value is 50-80% of the installed memory on the server. If this value is set too high, there will be no memory left for the operating system and other subsystems of MySQL, such as transaction logs. So, let's open our my.cnf file, search for innodb_buffer_pool_size, and set the value between the recommended value (that is, 50-80%) of our RAM.

innodb_buffer_pool_instances

This feature is not that widely used. It enables multiple buffer pool instances to work together to reduce the chances of memory contentions on a 64-bit system and with a large value for innodb_buffer_pool_size.

There are different choices on which the value for innodb_buffer_pool_instances are calculated. One way is to use one instance per GB of innodb_buffer_pool_size. So, if the value of innodb_bufer_pool_size is 16 GB, we will set innodb_buffer_pool_instances to 16.

innodb_log_file_size

The `innodb_log_file_size` is the the size of the log file that stores every query information executed. For a dedicated server, a value up to 4 GB is safe, but the time taken for crash recovery may increase if the log file's size is too large. So, in best practice, it is kept in between 1 and 4 GB.

The Percona Server - a fork of MySQL

According to the Percona website, Percona is a free, fully compatible, enhanced, open source, and drop-in replacement for MySQL that provides superior performance, scalability, and instrumentation.

Percona is a fork of MySQL with enhanced features for performance. All the features available in MySQL are available in Percona. Percona uses an enhanced storage engine called XtraDB. According to the Percona website, it is an enhanced version of the InnoDB storage engine for MySQL that has more features, faster performance, and better scalability on modern hardware. Percona XtraDB uses memory more efficiently in high-load environments.

As mentioned earlier, XtraDB is a fork of InnoDB, so all the features available in InnoDB are available in XtraDB.

Installing the Percona Server

Percona is only available for Linux systems. It is not available for Windows as of now. In this book, we will install Percona Server on Debian 8. The process is same for both Ubuntu and Debian.

 To install the Percona Server on other Linux flavors, check out the Percona installation manual at https://www.percona.com/doc/percona-server/5.5/installation.html. As of now, they provide instructions for Debian, Ubuntu, CentOS, and RHEL. They also provide instructions to install the Percona Server from sources and Git.

Now, let's install the Percona Server through the following steps:

1. Open your sources list file using the following command in your terminal:

   ```
   sudo nano /etc/apt/sources.list
   ```

   If prompted for a password, enter your Debian password. The file will be opened.

2. Now, place the following repository information at the end of the sources.list file:

   ```
   deb http://repo.percona.com/apt jessie main
   deb-src http://repo.percona.com/apt jessie main
   ```

3. Save the file by pressing *CTRL + O* and close the file by pressing *CTRL + X*.

4. Update your system using the following command in the terminal:

   ```
   sudo apt-get update
   ```

5. Start the installation by issuing the following command in the terminal:

   ```
   sudo apt-get install percona-server-server-5.5
   ```

6. The installation will be started. The process is the same as the MySQL server installation. During the installation, the root password for the Percona Server will be asked; you just need to enter it. When the installation is complete, you will be ready to use the Percona Server in the same way as MySQL.

7. Configure the Percona Server and optimize it as discussed in the earlier sections.

MySQL performance monitoring tools

There is always a need to monitor the performance of database servers. For this purpose, there are many tools available that make it easy to monitor MySQL servers and performance. Most of them are open source and free, and some provide a GUI. The command-line tools are more powerful and the best to use, though it takes a little time to understand and get used to them. We will discuss a few here.

phpMyAdmin

This is the most famous, web-based, open source, and free tool available to manage MySQL databases. Despite managing a MySQL server, it also provides some good tools to monitor a MySQL server. If we log in to phpMyAdmin and then click on the **Status** tab at the top, we will see the following screen:

The **Server** tab shows us basic data about the MySQL server, such as when it started, how much traffic is handled from the last start, information about connections, and so on.

The next is **Query Statistics**. This section provides full stats about all of the queries executed. It also provides a pie chart, which visualizes the percentage of each query type, as shown in the following screenshot.

If we carefully look at the chart, we can see that we have 54% of the SELECT queries running. If we use some kind of cache, such as Memcached or Redis, these SELECT queries should not be this high. So, this graph and statistics information provides us with a mean to analyze our cache systems.

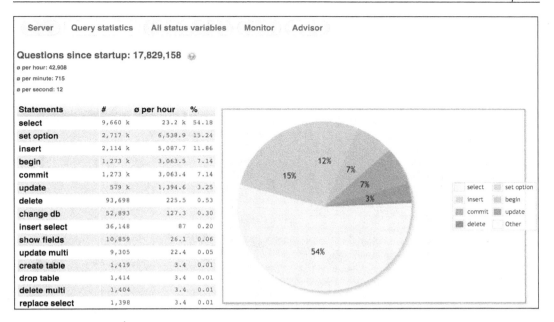

The next option is **All Status Variables**, which lists all of the MySQL variables and their current values. In this list, one can easily find out how MySQL is configured. In the following screenshot, our query cache variables and their values are shown:

Qcache free blocks	6.1 k	The number of free memo issuing a FLUSH QUERY
Qcache free memory	17 M	The amount of free memo
Qcache hits	261.1 M	The number of cache hits
Qcache inserts	9.4 M	The number of queries ad
Qcache lowmem prunes	5.6 M	The number of queries th help you tune the query c from the cache.
Qcache not cached	252.3 k	The number of non-cache
Qcache queries in cache	24 k	The number of queries re
Qcache total blocks	60.2 k	The total number of block
Queries	280.3 M	
Questions	280.3 M	

The next option that phpMyAdmin provides is **Monitor**. This is a very powerful tool that displays the server resources and their usages in real time in a graphical way.

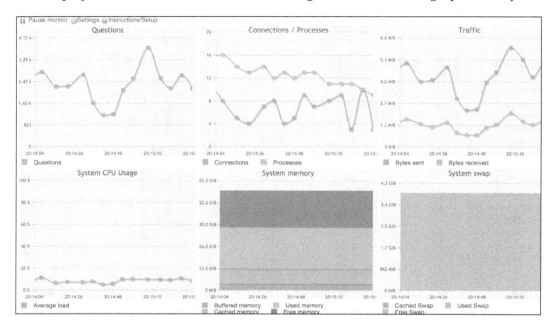

As shown in the preceding screenshot, we can see **Questions**, **Connections/Processes**, **System CPU Usage**, **Traffic**, **System Memory**, and **System swap** in a nice graphical interface.

The last important section is **Advisor**. This gives us advice regarding the settings for performance. It gives you as many details as possible so that the MySQL server can be tuned for performance. A small section from the advisor section is shown in the following screenshot:

Possible performance issues	
Issue	**Recommendation**
The MySQL manual only is accurate for official MySQL binaries.	Percona documentation is at http://www.percona.com/docs/wiki/
Suboptimal caching method.	You are using the MySQL Query cache with a fairly high traffic database. It might b especially if you have multiple slaves.
Cached queries are removed due to low query cache memory from the query cache.	You might want to increase query_cache_size, however keep in mind that the over small increments and monitor the results.
There are lots of rows being sorted.	While there is nothing wrong with a high amount of row sorting, you might want to r the ORDER BY clause, as this will result in much faster sorting
There are too many joins without indexes.	This means that joins are doing full table scans. Adding indexes for the columns be
The rate of reading the first index entry is high.	This usually indicates frequent full index scans. Full index scans are faster than tab had high volumes of UPDATEs and DELETEs, running 'OPTIMIZE TABLE' might r scans can only be reduced by rewriting queries.

If all these advices are applied, some performance can be gained.

The MySQL workbench

This is a desktop application from MySQL and is fully equipped with tools to manage and monitor the MySQL server. It provides us with a dashboard for performance in which all the data related to the server can be seen in a beautiful and graphical way, as shown in the screenshot that follows:

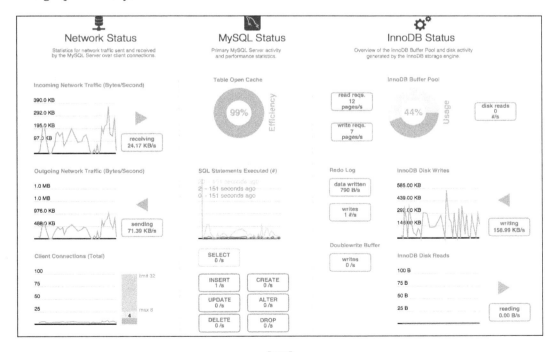

Percona Toolkit

All the tools mentioned before are good and provide some visual information about our database server. However, they are not good enough to show us some more useful information or provide more features that can make our lives easy. For this purpose, another command-line toolkit is available, which is called Percona Toolkit.

Percona Toolkit is a set of more than 30 command-line tools, which includes those used to do an analysis of slow queries, archive, optimize indices and many more.

 Percona Toolkit is free and open source and is available under GPL. Most of its tools run on Linux/Unix-based systems, but some can run on Windows too. An installation guide can be found at `https://www.percona.com/doc/percona-toolkit/2.2/installation.html`. A complete set of tools can be found at `https://www.percona.com/doc/percona-toolkit/2.2/index.html`.

Now, let's discuss a few tools in the subsections to follow.

pt-query-digest

This tool analyzes queries from slow, general, and binary log files. It generates a sophisticated report about the queries. Let's run this tool for slow queries using the following command:

```
Pt-query-digest /var/log/mysql/mysql-slow.log
```

After entering the preceding command in the terminal, we will see a long report. Here, we will discuss a short part of the report, as shown in the following screenshot:

```
# Profile
# Rank Query ID           Response time      Calls R/Call  V/M   Item
# ==== ================== ================== ===== ======= ===== =======
#    1 0xCEB312D0FA1C37CE 10683.7659 11.9%    165 64.7501 70.89 SELECT
#    2 0xA836779D3D007C7C 10323.4901 11.5%    142 72.7006 92.79 SELECT
#    3 0x0C7EA293C3196265  9889.3175 11.0%    147 67.2743 14... SELECT
#    4 0xD70662D2ECA11099  8618.3030  9.6%    147 58.6279 14... SELECT
#    5 0xEE6E30152233C978  5687.1127  6.3%    134 42.4411 38.55 SELECT
#    6 0x7C28ED0781B7DC05  5220.0295  5.8%    129 40.4653 41.13 SELECT
#    7 0x813031B8BBC3B329  4895.0396  5.4%   2926  1.6729  0.19 COMMIT
#    8 0x71CE1B0B17DCC70F  3179.1896  3.5%    151 21.0542 19.94 SELECT
#    9 0x1E3F38720A7F9E01  2805.9224  3.1%    126 22.2692 21.57 SELECT
#   10 0x86485AAB2E3523AB  1951.5777  2.2%    374  5.2181 18.41 INSERT
#   11 0x5F9B42BF4A256B2E  1806.6999  2.0%     69 26.1841 10.16 INSERT
#   12 0x2CE0A1392B331E05  1713.9884  1.9%    558  3.0717  4.03 SELECT
```

In the preceding screenshot, slow queries are listed with the slowest at the top. The first query, which is a SELECT query, takes the most time, which is about 12% of the total time. The second query, which is also a SELECT query, takes 11.5% of the total time. From this report, we can see which queries are slow so that we can optimize them for the best performance.

Also, pt-query-digest displays information for each query, as shown in the following screenshot. In the screenshot, data about the first query is mentioned, including the total timing; percentage (pct) of time; min, max, and average time; bytes sent; and some other parameters:

```
# Query 1: 0.00 QPS, 0.00x concurrency, ID 0xCEB312D0FA1C37CE at byte 7534347
# This item is included in the report because it matches --limit.
# Scores: V/M = 70.89
# Time range: 2014-12-21 11:14:08 to 2015-11-14 11:24:17
# Attribute     pct    total     min     max     avg     95%  stddev  median
# ============ === ======= ======= ======= ======= ======= ======= =======
# Count          0     165
# Exec time     11  10684s      5s    647s     65s    159s     68s     45s
# Lock time      0    16ms       0   184us    94us   144us    23us    84us
# Rows sent     10  47.61M       0 368.14k 295.45k 362.29k  66.84k 298.06k
# Rows examine   5  47.61M       0 368.14k 295.45k 362.29k  66.84k 298.06k
# Rows affecte   0       0       0       0       0       0       0       0
# Bytes sent    13   1.20G   2.77M  31.57M   7.46M   8.03M   5.35M   7.29M
# Merge passes   0       0       0       0       0       0       0       0
# Tmp tables     0       0       0       0       0       0       0       0
# Tmp disk tbl   0       0       0       0       0       0       0       0
# Tmp tbl size   0       0       0       0       0       0       0       0
# Query size     0   8.70k      54      54      54      54       0      54
# InnoDB:
```

pt-duplicate-key-checker

This tool finds duplicate indices and duplicate foreign keys either in a set of specified tables or in a complete database. Let's execute this tool again in a large database using the following command in the terminal:

```
Pt-duplicate-key-checker –user packt –password dbPassword –database
packt_pub
```

When executed, the following output is printed:

```
# ####################################################################
# ███████████_live.widget_instance_page_layout
# ####################################################################

# IDX_WIDGET_INSTANCE_PAGE_LAYOUT_LAYOUT_UPDATE_ID is a left-prefix of UNQ_WIDGET_INSTANCE_PAGE_LAYOUT_LAYOUT_UPDATE_ID_PAGE_ID
# Key definitions:
#   KEY `IDX_WIDGET_INSTANCE_PAGE_LAYOUT_LAYOUT_UPDATE_ID` (`layout_update_id`),
#   UNIQUE KEY `UNQ_WIDGET_INSTANCE_PAGE_LAYOUT_LAYOUT_UPDATE_ID_PAGE_ID` (`layout_update_id`,`page_id`),
# Column types:
#         `layout_update_id` int(10) unsigned not null default '0' comment 'layout update id'
#         `page_id` int(10) unsigned not null default '0' comment 'page id'
# To remove this duplicate index, execute:
ALTER TABLE `███████████_live`.`widget_instance_page_layout` DROP INDEX `IDX_WIDGET_INSTANCE_PAGE_LAYOUT_LAYOUT_UPDATE_ID`;

# ####################################################################
# Summary of indexes
# ####################################################################

# Size Duplicate Indexes    361243847
# Total Duplicate Indexes   84
# Total Indexes             1719
----------------------------------------------------------------
```

At the end of the report, a summary of the indices is displayed, which is
self-explanatory. Also, this tool prints out an ALTER query for each duplicate
index that can be executed as a MySQL query to fix the index, as follows:

Pt-variable-advisor

This tool displays MySQL config information and advice for each query. This is a
good tool that can help us set up MySQL configurations properly. We can execute
this tool by running the following command:

Pt-variable-advisor -user packt -password DbPassword localhost

After execution, the following output will be displayed:

```
# NOTE connect_timeout: A large value of this setting can create a denial of service vulnerability.

# WARN delay_key_write: MyISAM index blocks are never flushed until necessary.

# WARN innodb_additional_mem_pool_size: This variable generally doesn't need to be larger than 20MB.

# WARN innodb_fast_shutdown: InnoDB's shutdown behavior is not the default.

# WARN innodb_flush_log_at_trx_commit-1: InnoDB is not configured in strictly ACID mode.

# WARN innodb_log_buffer_size: The InnoDB log buffer size generally should not be set larger than 16MB.

# NOTE log_warnings-2: Log_warnings must be set greater than 1 to log unusual events such as aborted connections.

# NOTE max_binlog_size: The max_binlog_size is smaller than the default of 1GB.
```

There are many other tools provided by Percona Toolkit that are out of the scope
of this book. However, the documentation at https://www.percona.com/doc/
percona-toolkit/2.2/index.html is very helpful and easy to understand.
It provides complete details for each tool, including its description and risks,
how to execute it, and other options if there are any. This documentation is
worth reading if you wish to understand any tool in Percona Toolkit.

Percona XtraDB Cluster (PXC)

Percona XtraDB Cluster provides a high-performance cluster environment that can help easily configure and manage a database on multiple servers. It enables databases to communicate with each other using the binary logs. The cluster environment helps divide the load among different database servers and provides safety from failure in case a server is down.

To set up the cluster, we need the following servers:

- One server with IP 10.211.55.1, which we will call Node1

- A second server with IP 10.211.55.2, which we will call Node2

- And a third server with IP 10.211.55.3, which we will call Node3

As we already have the Percona repository in our sources, let's start by installing and configuring Percona XtraDB Cluster, also called PXC. Perform the following steps:

1. First, install Percona XtraDB Cluster on Node1 by issuing the following command in the terminal:

   ```
   apt-get install percona-xtradb-cluster-56
   ```

   The installation will start similarly to a normal Percona Server installation. During the installation, the password for a root user will be also asked.

2. When the installation is complete, we need to create a new user that has replication privileges. Issue the following commands in the MySQL terminal after logging in to it:

   ```
   CREATE USER 'sstpackt'@'localhost' IDENTIFIED BY
   'sstuserpassword';
   GRANT RELOAD, LOCK TABLES, REPLICATION CLIENT ON *.* TO
   'sstpackt'@'localhost';
   FLUSH PRIVILEGES;
   ```

   The first query creates a user with the username sstpackt and password sstuserpassword. The username and password can be anything, but a good and strong password is recommended. The second query sets proper privileges to our new user, including locking tables and replication. The third query refreshes the privileges.

3. Now, open the MySQL configuration file located at /etc/mysql/my.cnf. Then, place the following configuration in the mysqld block:

   ```
   #Add the galera library
   wsrep_provider=/usr/lib/libgalera_smm.so
   ```

```
#Add cluster nodes addresses
wsrep_cluster_address=gcomm://10.211.55.1,10.211.55.2,
10.211.55.3

#The binlog format should be ROW. It is required for galera to
work properly
binlog_format=ROW

#default storage engine for mysql will be InnoDB
default_storage_engine=InnoDB

#The InnoDB auto increment lock mode should be 2, and it is
required for galera
innodb_autoinc_lock_mode=2

#Node 1 address
wsrep_node_address=10.211.55.1

#SST method
wsrep_sst_method=xtrabackup

#Authentication for SST method. Use the same user name and
password created in above step 2
wsrep_sst_auth="sstpackt:sstuserpassword"

#Give the cluster a name
wsrep_cluster_name=packt_cluster
```

Save the file after adding the preceding configuration.

4. Now, start the first node by issuing the following command:

   /etc/init.d/mysql bootstrap-pxc

   This will bootstrap the first node. Bootstrapping means getting the initial cluster up and running and defining which node has the correct information and which one all the other nodes should sync to. As Node1 is our initial cluster node and we created a new user here, we have to only bootstrap Node1.

> **SST** stands for **State Snapshot Transfer**. It is responsible for copying full data from one node to another. It is only used when a new node is added to the cluster and this node has to get complete initial data from an existing node. Three SST methods are available in Percona XtraDB Cluster, mysqldump, rsync, and xtrabackup.

5. Log in to the MySQL terminal on the first node and issue the following command:

```
SHOW STATUS LIKE '%wsrep%';
```

A very long list will be displayed. A few of them are shown in the following screenshot:

```
mysql> show status like '%wsrep_cluster%';
+--------------------------+--------------------------------------+
| Variable_name            | Value                                |
+--------------------------+--------------------------------------+
| wsrep_cluster_conf_id    | 1                                    |
| wsrep_cluster_size       | 1                                    |
| wsrep_cluster_state_uuid | 65925905-f650-11e5-b9a4-b3804a801699 |
| wsrep_cluster_status     | Primary                              |
+--------------------------+--------------------------------------+
4 rows in set (0.00 sec)

mysql>
```

6. Now, repeat Step 1 and Step 3 for all nodes. The only configuration that needs to be changed for each node is `wsrep_node_address`, which should be the IP address of the node. Edit the `my.cnf` configuration file for all the nodes and place the node address in `wsrep_node_address`.

7. Start the two new nodes by issuing the following command in the terminal:

```
/etc/init.d/mysql start
```

Now each node can be verified by repeating step 7.

To verify whether the cluster is working fine, create a database in one node and add some tables and data into the tables. After this, check other nodes for the newly created database, tables, and the data entered in each table. We will have all this data synced to each node.

Redis – the key-value cache store

Redis is an open source, in-memory key-value data store that is widely used for database caching. According to the Redis website (www.Redis.io), Redis supports data structures such as strings, hashes, lists, sets, and sorted lists. Also, Redis supports replication and transactions.

> Redis installation instructions can be found at
> http://redis.io/topics/quickstart.

To check whether Redis is working fine on your server or not, start the Redis server instance by running the following command in the terminal:

```
redis server
```

Then issue the following command in a different terminal window:

```
redis-cli ping
```

If the output of the preceding command is as follows, the Redis server is ready to be run:

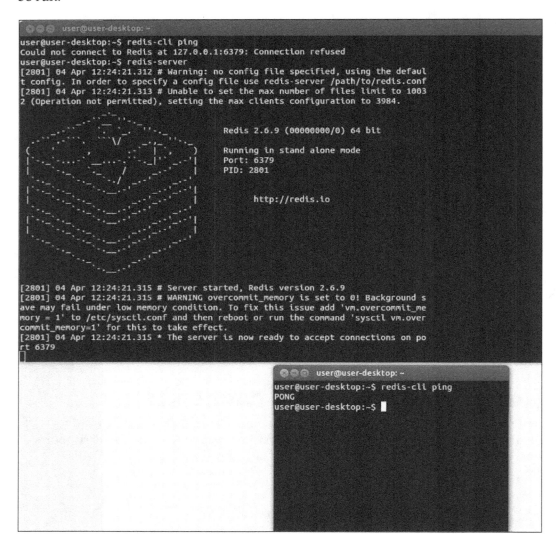

Redis provides a command line, which provides some useful commands. There are two ways to execute commands on the Redis server. You can either use the previous method or just type `redis-cli` and hit *Enter*; we will be presented with the Redis command line, where we can then just type the Redis commands that will be executed.

By default, Redis uses the IP 127.0.0.1 and port 6379. Remote connections are not allowed, though remote connections can be enabled. Redis stores data that is already created in the database. Database names are integer numbers, such as 0, 1, 2, and so on.

We won't go in much detail about Redis here, but we will discuss a few commands that are worth noting. Note that all these commands can be either executed in the previous way, or we can just enter the `redis-cli` command window and type the commands without typing `redis-cli`. Also, the following commands can be executed directly in PHP, which makes it possible to clear out the cache directly from our PHP application:

- `SELECT`: This command changes the current database. By default, redis-cli will be opened at database 0. So, if we want to go to database 1, we will run the following command:

  `SELECT 1`

- `FLUSHDB`: This command flushes the current database. All keys or data from the current database will be deleted.

- `FLUSHALL`: This command flushes all the databases, no matter which database it is executed in.

- `KEYS`: This command lists all the keys in the current database matching a pattern. The following command lists all the keys in the current database.

  `KEYS *`

Now, it's time for some action in PHP with Redis.

 As of writing this topic, PHP 7 does not have built-in support for Redis yet. For this book's purpose, we compiled the PHPRedis module for PHP 7, and it works very nicely. The module can be found at `https://github.com/phpredis/phpredis`.

Connecting with the Redis server

As mentioned before, by default, the Redis server runs on the IP 127.0.0.1 and port 6379. So, to make a connection, we will use these details. Take a look at the following code:

```
$redisObject = new Redis();
if( !$redisObject->connect('127.0.0.1', 6379))
  die("Can't connect to Redis Server");
```

In the first line, we instantiated a Redis object by the name of `redisObject`, which is then used in the second line to connect to the Redis server. The host is the local IP address 127.0.0.1, and the port is 6379. The `connect()` method returns `TRUE` if the connection is successful; otherwise, it returns `FALSE`.

Storing and fetching data from the Redis server

Now, we are connected to our Redis server. Let's save some data in the Redis database. For our example, we want to store some string data in the Redis database. The code is as follows:

```
//Use same code as above for connection.
//Save Data in to Redis database.
$rdisObject->set('packt_title', 'Packt Publishing');

//Lets get our data from database
echo $redisObject->get('packt_title');
```

The `set` method stores data into the current Redis database and takes two arguments: a key and a value. A key can be any unique name, and a value is what we need to store. So, our key is `packt_title`, and the value is `Packt Publishing`. The default database is always set to 0 (zero) unless explicitly set otherwise. So, the preceding `set` method will save our data to database 0 with the `packt_title` key.

Now, the `get` method is used to fetch data from the current database. It takes the key as the argument. So, the output of the preceding code will be our saved string data `Packt Publishing`.

Now, what about arrays or a set of data coming from the database? We can store them in several ways in Redis. Let's first try the normal strings way, as shown here:

```
//Use same connection code as above.

/* This $array can come from anywhere, either it is coming from
database or user entered form data or an array defined in code */

$array = ['PHP 5.4', PHP 5.5, 'PHP 5.6', PHP 7.0];

//Json encode the array
$encoded = json_encode($array);

//Select redis database 1
$redisObj->select(1);

//store it in redis database 1
$redisObject->set('my_array', $encoded);

//Now lets fetch it
$data = $redisObject->get('my_array');

//Decode it to array
$decoded = json_decode($data, true);

print_r($decoded);
```

The output of the preceding code will be the same array. For testing purposes, we can comment out the set method and check whether the get method fetches the data or not. Remember that in the preceding code, we stored the array as a json string, then fetched it as a json string, and decoded it to the array. This is because we used the methods that are available for the string datatype, and it is not possible to store arrays in the string datatype.

Also, we used the select method to select another database and use it instead of 0. This data will be stored in database 1 and can't be fetched if we are at database 0.

> A complete discussion of Redis is out of the scope of this book. So, we have provided an introduction. Note that if you use any framework, you have built-in libraries available for Redis that are easy to use, and any datatype can be used easily.

Redis management tools

Redis management tools provide an easy way to manage Redis databases. These tools provide features so that every key can be checked and a cache can be cleared easily. One default tool comes with Redis, called Redis-cli, and we discussed it earlier. Now, let's discuss a visual tool that is great and easy to use, called **Redis Desktop Manage** (**RDM**). A screenshot of the main window of RDM looks like the following screenshot:

RDM provides the following features:

- It connects to remote multiple Redis servers
- It displays data in a specific key in different formats
- It adds new keys to a selected database
- It adds more data to a selected key
- It edits/deletes keys and their names
- It supports SSH and SSL and is cloud ready

There are some other tools that can be used, but RDM and Redis-cli are the best and easiest to use.

Memcached key-value cache store

According to the Memcached official website, it's a free, open source, high performance, and distributed memory object caching system. Memcached is an in-memory key-value store that can store datasets from a database or API calls.

Similarly to Redis, Memcached also helps a lot in speeding up a website. It stores the data (strings or objects) in the memory. This allows us to reduce the communication with outside resources, such as databases and or APIs.

 We are assuming that Memcached is installed on the server. Also, the PHP extension for PHP 7 is also assumed to be installed.

Now, let's play a little with Memcachd in PHP. Take a look at the following code:

```php
//Instantiate Memcached Object
$memCached = new Memcached();

//Add server
$memCached->addServer('127.0.0.1', 11211);

//Lets get some data
$data = $memCached->get('packt_title');

//Check if data is available
if($data)
{
  echo $data;
}
else
{
  /*No data is found. Fetch your data from any where and add to
memcached */

  $memCached->set('packt_title', 'Packt Publishing');

}
```

The preceding code is a very simple example of using Memcached. The comments are written with each line of code and are self-explanatory. After instantiating a Memcached object, we have to add a Memcached server. By default, the Memcached server server runs on the localhost IP, which is 127.0.0.1, and on the port 11211. After this, we checked for some data using a key, and if it is available, we can process it (in this case, we displayed it. It can be returned, or whatever processing is required can be carried out.). If the data is not available, we can just add it. Please note that the data can come from a remote server API or from the database.

 We have just provided an introduction to Memcached and how it can help us store data and improve performance. A complete discussion is not possible in this title. A good book on Memcached is *Getting Started with Memcached* by Packt Publishing.

Summary

In this chapter, we covered MySQL and the Percona Server. Also, we discussed in detail query caching and other MySQL configuration options for performance in detail. We mentioned different storage engines, such as MyISAM, InnoDB, and Percona XtraDB. We also configured Percona XtraDB Cluster on three nodes. We discussed different monitoring tools, such as PhpMyAdmin monitoring tools, MySQL workbench performance monitoring, and Percona Toolkit. We also discussed Redis and Memcached caching for PHP and MySQL.

In the next chapter, we will discuss benchmarking and different tools. We will use XDebug, Apache JMeter, ApacheBench, and Siege to benchmark different open source systems, such as WordPress, Magento, Drupal, and different versions of PHP, and compare their performance with PHP 7.

5
Debugging and Profiling

During development, every developer faces problems, and it becomes unclear what is really going on here and why the problem is generated. Most the time, these issues can be logical or with the data. It is always hard to find such issues. Debugging is a process to find such issues and problems and fix them. Similarly, we often need to know how many resources a script consumes, including memory consumption, CPU, and how much time it takes to execute.

In this chapter, we will cover the following topics:

- Xdebug
- Debugging with Sublime Text 3
- Debugging with Eclipse
- Profiling with Xdebug
- PHP DebugBar

Xdebug

Xdebug is an extension for PHP that provides both debugging and profiling information for PHP scripts. Xdebug displays a full-stake trace information for errors, including function names, line numbers, and filenames. Also, it provides the ability to debug scripts interactively using different IDEs, such as Sublime Text, Eclipse, PHP Storm, and Zend Studio.

To check whether Xdebug is installed and enabled on our PHP installation, we need to check the phpinfo() details. On the phpinfo details page, search for Xdebug, and you should see details similar to the following screenshot:

This program makes use of the Zend Scripting Language Engine:
Zend Engine v3.0.0, Copyright (c) 1998-2016 Zend Technologies
    with Zend OPcache v7.0.6-dev, Copyright (c) 1999-2016, by Zend Technologies
    with Xdebug v2.4.0RC4, Copyright (c) 2002-2016, by Derick Rethans

zend engine

This means that our PHP installation has Xdebug installed. Now, we need to configure Xdebug. Either the Xdebug configuration will be in the php.ini file, or it will have its separate .ini file. At our installation, we will have a separate 20-xdebug.ini file placed at the /etc/php/7.0/fpm/conf.d/ path.

> For the purpose of this book, we will use the Homestead Vagrant box from Laravel. It provides complete tools on the Ubuntu 14.04 LTS installation, including PHP7 with Xdebug, NGINX, and MySQL. For the purpose of development, this Vagrant box is a perfect solution. More information can be found at https://laravel.com/docs/5.1/homestead.

Now, open the 20-xdebug.ini file and place the following configuration in it:

```
zend_extension = xdebug.so
xdebug.remote_enable = on
xdebug.remote_connect_back = on
xdebug.idekey = "vagrant"
```

The preceding are the minimum configurations we should use that enable remote debugging and set an IDE key. Now, restart PHP by issuing the following command in the terminal:

```
sudo service php-fpm7.0 restart
```

Now we are ready to debug some code.

Debugging with Sublime Text

The Sublime Text editor has a plugin that can be used to debug PHP code with Xdebug. First, let's install the xdebug package for Sublime Text.

> For this topic, we will use Sublime Text 3, which is still in beta. It is your own choice to use version 2 or 3.

First, go to **Tools | Command Pallet**. A popup similar to the following will be displayed:

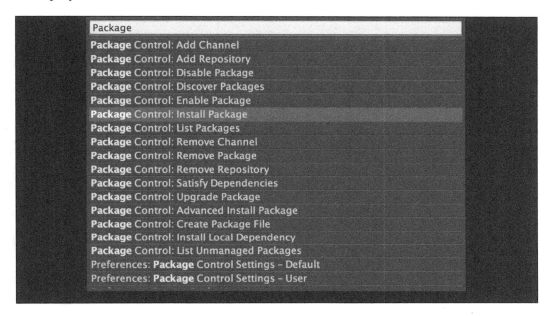

Select **Package Control: Install Package**, and a popup similar to the following screenshot will be displayed:

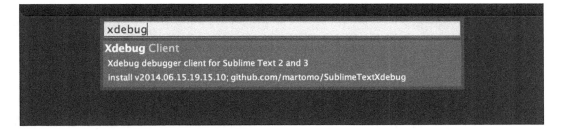

Type in xdebug, and the **Xdebug Client** package will be displayed. Click on it and wait for a while until it is installed.

Now, create a project in Sublime Text and save it. Open the Sublime Text project file and insert the following code in it:

```
{
    "folders":
    [
        {
```

```
          "follow_symlinks": true,
          "path": "."
        }
    ],

    "settings": {
      "xdebug": {
        "path_mapping": {
        "full_path_on_remote_host" : "full_path_on_local_host"
        },
        "url" : http://url-of-application.com/,
        "super_globals" : true,
        "close_on_stop" : true,
        }
      }
    }
```

The highlighted code is important, and it has to be entered for Xdebug. Path mapping is the most important part. It should have a full path to the root of the application on the remote host and a full path to the root of the application on the localhost.

Now, let's start debugging. Create a file at the project's root, name it `index.php`, and place the following code in it:

```
$a = [1,2,3,4,5];
$b = [4,5,6,7,8];

$c = array_merge($a, $b);
```

Now, right-click on a line in the editor and select **Xdebug**. Then, click on **Add/Remove Breakpoint**. Let's add a few breakpoints as shown in the following screenshot:

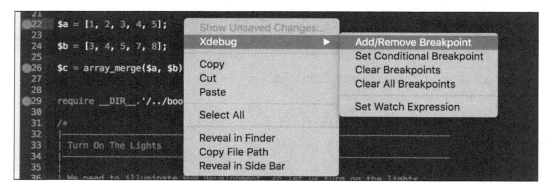

When a breakpoint is added to a line, a filled circle will be displayed on the left-hand side near the line number, as can be seen in the preceding screenshot.

Now we are ready to debug our PHP code. Navigate to **Tools | Xdebug | Start Debugging (Launch in Browser)**. A browser window will open the application along with a Sublime Text debug session parameter. The browser windows will be in the loading state because as soon as the first breakpoint is reached, the execution stops. The browser window will be similar to the following:

Some new small windows will also open in the Sublime Text editor that will display debugging information along with all the variables available, as in the following screenshot:

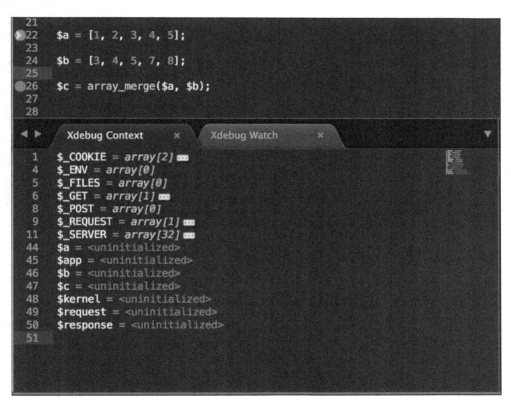

In the preceding screenshot, our $a, $b, and $c arrays are uninitialized because the execution cursor is at Line 22, and it has stopped there. Also, all server variables, cookies, environment variables, request data, and POST and GET data can be seen here. This way, we can debug all kind of variables, arrays, and objects and check what data each variable, object, or array holds at a certain point. This gives us the possibility to find out the errors that are very hard to detect without debugging.

Now, let's move the execution cursor ahead. Right-click in the editor code section and go to **Xdebug | Step Into**. The cursor will move ahead, and the variables data may change according to the next line. This can be noted in the following screenshot:

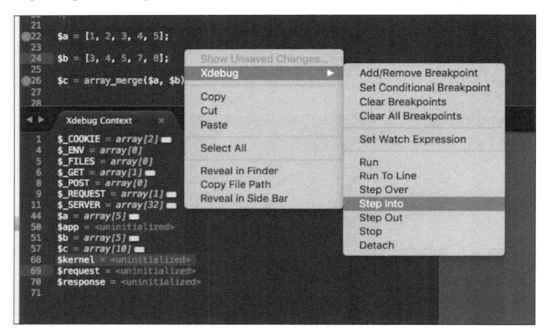

Debugging can be stopped by clicking on **Tools | Xdebug | Stop Debugging**.

Debugging with Eclipse

Eclipse is the most free and powerful IDE widely used. It supports almost all major programming languages, including PHP. We will discuss how to configure Eclipse to use Xdebug to debug.

First, open the project in Eclipse. Then, click on the down arrow to the right of the small bug icon in the tool bar, as shown in the following screenshot:

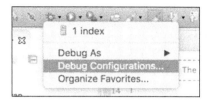

After this, click on the **Debug Configuration** menu, and the following windows will open:

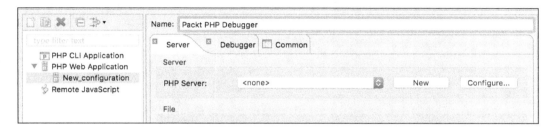

Select **PHP Web Application** on left panel and then click on the **Add New** icon in the top-left corner. This will add a new configuration, as shown in the preceding screenshot. Give the configuration a name. Now, we need to add a PHP server to our configuration. Click on the **New** button on the right-hand side panel, and the following window will open:

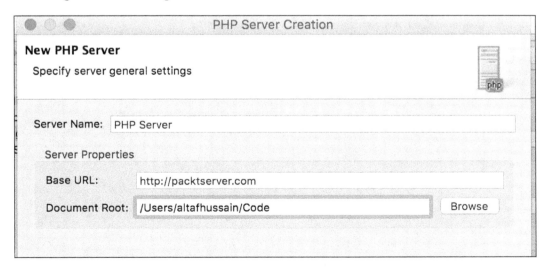

We will enter the server name as `PHP Server`. The server name can be anything as long as it is user-friendly and can be recognized for later use. In the **Base URL** field, enter the complete URL of the application. **Document Root** should be the local path of the root of the application. After entering all the valid data, click on the **Next** button, and we will see the following window:

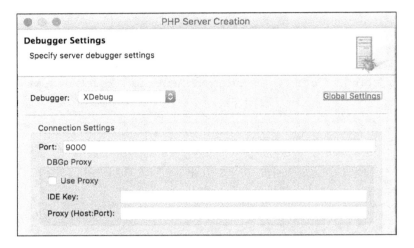

Select **XDebug** in the **Debugger** drop-down list and leave rest of the fields as they are. Click on the **Next** button, and we will have the path mapping window. It is very important to map the correct local path to the correct remote path. Click on the **Add** button, and we will have the following window:

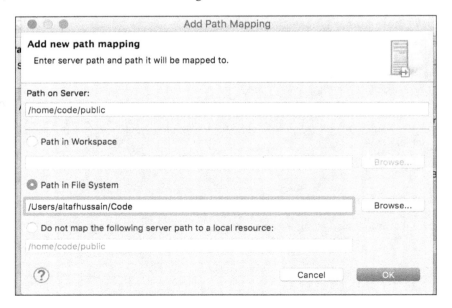

Enter the full path to the document root of the application on the remote server. Then, select **Path in File System** and enter the local path of the application's document root. Click on **OK** and then click on the **Finish** button in the path mapping window. Then, click on **Finish** in the next window to complete adding a PHP server.

Now, our configuration is ready. First, we will add some breakpoints to our PHP file by clicking on the line number bar and a small blue dot will appear there, as shown in the following screenshot. Now, click on the small bug icon on the tool bar, select **Debug As**, and then click on **PHP Web Application**. The debug process will start, and a window will be opened in the browser. It will be in the loading state, same as we saw in Sublime Text debugging. Also, the Debug perspective will be opened in Eclipse, as shown here:

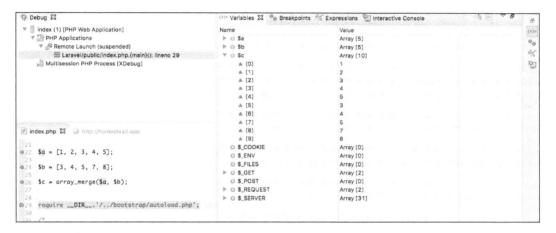

When we click on the small (**X**)= icon in the right-hand side bar, we will see all the variables there. Also, it is possible to edit any variable data, even the element values of any array, object properties, and cookie data. The modified data will be retained for the current debug session.

To step into the next line, we will just press *F5*, and the execution cursor will be moved to the next line. To step out to the next breakpoint, we will press *F6*.

Profiling with Xdebug

Profiling gives us information about the cost of each script or task executed in an application. It helps to provide information about how much time a task takes, and hence we can optimize our code to consume less time.

Xdebug has a profiler that is disabled by default. To enable the profiler, open the configuration file and place the following two lines in it:

```
xdebug.profiler_enable=on
xdebug.profiler_output_dir=/var/xdebug/profiler/
```

The first line enables the profiler. The second line, where we defined the output directory for the profiler file, is important. In this directory, Xdebug will store the output file when the profiler is executed. The output file is stored with a name, such as `cachegrind.out.id`. This file contains all the profile data in a simple text format.

Now, we are set to profile a simple installation of the Laravel application home page. The installation is a fresh and clean one. Now, let's open the application in a browser and append `?XDEBUG_PROFILE=on` at the end, as shown here:

`http://application_url.com?XDEBUG_PROFILE=on`

After this page is loaded, a `cachegrind` file will be generated at the specified location. Now, when we open the file in a text editor, we will just see some text data.

 The `cachegrind` file can be opened with different tools. One of the tools for Windows is WinCacheGrind. For Mac, we have qcachegrind. Any of these applications will view the file data in such a way that we will see all the data in an interactive form that can be easily analyzed. Also, PHP Storm has a nice analyzer for cachegrind. For this topic, we used PHP Storm IDE.

After opening the file in PHP Storm, we will get a window similar to the following screenshot:

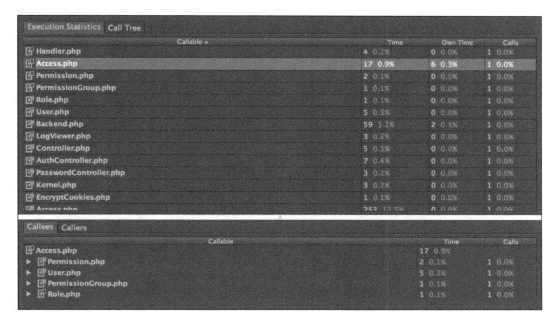

As shown in the preceding screenshot, we have execution statistics in the upper pane that shows the time (in ms) taken by each called script individually along with the number of times it is called. In the lower pane, we have the callees that called this script.

We can analyze which script takes more time, and we can optimize this script to reduce its execution time. Also, we can find out whether, at a certain point, we need to call a specific script or not. If not, then we can remove this call.

PHP DebugBar

PHP DebugBar is another awesome tool that displays a nice and full information bar at the bottom of the page. It can display custom messages added for the purposes of debugging and full request information including $_COOKIE, $_SERVER, $_POST, and $_GET arrays along with the data if any of them have. Besides that, PHP DebugBar displays details about exceptions if there are any, database queries executed, and their details. Also it displays the memory taken by the script and the time the page is loaded in.

According to the PHP Debug website, DebugBar integrates easily in any application project and displays debugging and profiling data from any part of the application.

Its installation is easy. You can either download the complete source code, place it somewhere in your application, and set up the autoloader to load all the classes, or use composer to install it. We will use composer as it is the easy and clean way to install it.

Composer is a nice tool for PHP to manage the dependencies of a project. It is written in PHP and is freely available from https://getcomposer.org/. We assume that composer is installed on your machine.

In your project's composer.json file, place the following code in the required section:

```
"maximebf/debugbar" : ">=1.10.0"
```

Save the file and then issue the following command:

```
composer update
```

The Composer will start updating the dependencies and install composer. Also, it will generate the autoloader file and/or the other dependencies required for DebugBar.

The preceding composer command will only work if composer is installed globally on the system. If it is not, we have to use the following command:

```
php composer.phar update
```

The preceding command should be executed in the folder where composer.phar is placed.

After it is installed, the project tree for the DebugBar can be as follows:

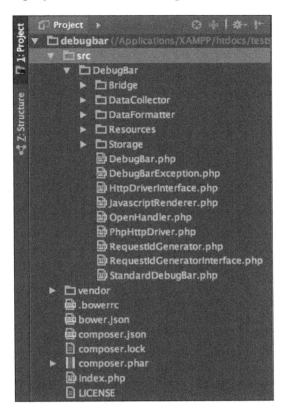

The directories' structure may be a little bit different, but normally, it will be as we previously noted. The `src` directory has the complete source code for DebugBar. The `vendor` directory has some third-party modules or PHP tools that may or may not be required. Also, note that the `vendor` folder has the autoloader to autoload all the classes.

Let's check our installation now to see whether it is working or not. Create a new file in your project root and name it `index.php`. After this, place the following code in it:

```php
<?php
require "vendor/autoloader.php";
use Debugbar\StandardDebugBar;
$debugger = new StandardDebugBar();
$debugbarRenderer = $debugbar->getJavascriptRenderer();
```

```
//Add some messages
$debugbar['messages']->addMessage('PHP 7 by Packt');
$debugbar['messages']->addMessage('Written by Altaf Hussain');

?>

<html>
  <head>
    <?php echo $debugbarRenderer->renderHead(); ?>
  </head>
  <title>Welcome to Debug Bar</title>
  <body>
    <h1>Welcome to Debug Bar</h1>

  <!—- display debug bar here -->
  <?php echo $debugbarRenderer->render();  ?>

  </body>
</html>
```

In the preceding code, we first included our autoloader, which is generated by composer for us to autoload all the classes. Then, we used the DebugBar\ StandardDebugbar namespace. After this, we instantiated two objects: StandardDebugBar and getJavascriptRenderer. The StandardDebugBar object is an array of objects that has objects for different collectors, such as message collectors and others. The getJavascriptRenderer object is responsible for placing the required JavaScript and CSS code at the header and displaying the bar at the bottom of the page.

We used the $debugbar object to add messages to the message collector. Collectors are responsible for collecting data from different sources, such as databases, HTTP requests, messages, and others.

In the head section of the HTML code, we used the renderHead method of $debugbarRenderer to place the required JavaScript and CSS code. After this, just before the end of the <body> block, we used the render method of the same object to display the debug bar.

Now, load the application in the browser, and if you notice a bar at the bottom of the browser as in the following screenshot, then congrats! DebugBar is properly installed and is working fine.

On the right-hand side, we have the memory consumed by our application and the time it is loaded in.

If we click on the **Messages** tab, we will see the messages we added, as shown in the following screenshot:

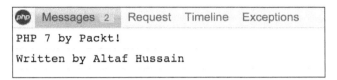

DebugBar provides data collectors, which are used to collect data from different sources. These are called *base collectors*, and some of the data collectors are as follows:

- The message collector collects log messages, as shown in the preceding example
- The TimeData collector collects the total execution time as well as the execution time for a specific operation
- The exceptions collector displays all the exceptions that have occurred
- The PDO collector logs SQL queries
- The RequestData collector collects data of PHP global variables, such as $_SERVER, $_POST, $_GET, and others
- The config collector is used to display any key-value pairs of arrays

Also, there are some collectors that provide the ability to collect data from third-party frameworks such as Twig, Swift Mailer, Doctrine, and others. These collectors are called bridge collectors. PHP DebugBar can be easily integrated into famous PHP frameworks such as Laravel and Zend Framework 2 too.

A complete discussion of PHP DebugBar is not possible in this book. Therefore, only a simple introduction is provided here. PHP DebugBar has a nice documentation that provides complete details with examples. The documentation can be found at http://phpdebugbar.com/docs/readme.html.

Summary

In this chapter, we discussed different tools to debug a PHP application. We used Xdebug, Sublime Text 3, and Eclipse to debug our applications. Then, we used the Xdebug profiler to profile an application to find out the execution statistics. Finally, we discussed PHP DebugBar to debug an application.

In the next chapter, we will discuss load testing tools, which we can use to place load or virtual visitors on our application in order to load test it, and find out how much load our application can bear, and how it affects the performance.

6
Stress/Load Testing PHP Applications

After an application is developed, tested, debugged and then profiled, it is time to bring it to production. However, before going to production, it is best practice to stress/load test the application. This test will give us an approximate result of how many requests at a certain time can be handled by our server running the application. Using these results, we can optimize the application, web server, database, and our caching tools to get a better result and process more requests.

In this chapter, we will load test different open source tools on both PHP 5.6 and PHP 7 and compare these applications' performance for both versions of PHP.

We will cover the following topics:

- Apache JMeter
- ApacheBench (ab)
- Seige
- Load testing Magento 2 on PHP 5.6 and PHP 7
- Load testing WordPress on PHP 5.6 and PHP 7
- Load testing Drupal 8 on PHP 5.6 and PHP 7

Apache JMeter

Apache JMeter is a graphical and open source tool used to load test a server's performance. JMeter is completely written in Java, so it is compatible with all operating systems that have Java installed. JMeter has a complete set of extensive tools for every kind of load testing, from static content to dynamic resources and web services.

Its installation is simple. We need to download it from the JMeter website and then just run the application. As mentioned before, it will require Java to be installed on the machine.

> JMeter can test FTP servers, mail servers, database servers, queries, and more. In this book, we can't cover all these topics, so we will only load test web servers. Apache JMeter's list of features can be found at
> http://jmeter.apache.org/.

When we run the application at first, we will see the following window:

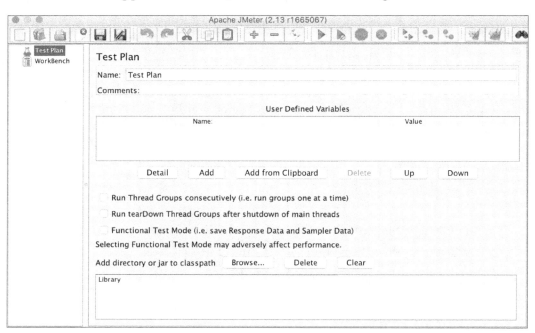

To run any kind of test, you need to first create a test plan. A test plan has all the components required to execute this test. By default, JMeter has a test plan called Test Plan. Let's name it to our own plan, `Packt Publisher Test Plan`, as shown in the following screenshot:

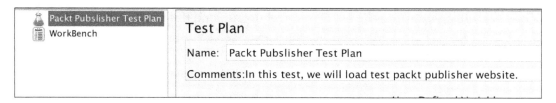

Now, save the test plan, and JMeter we will create a `.jmx` file. Save it in an appropriate place.

The next step is to add a thread group. *A thread group defines some basic properties for the test plan, which can be common among all types of tests.* To add a thread group, right-click on the plan in the left panel, then navigate to **Add | Threads (Users) | Thread Group**. The following window will be displayed:

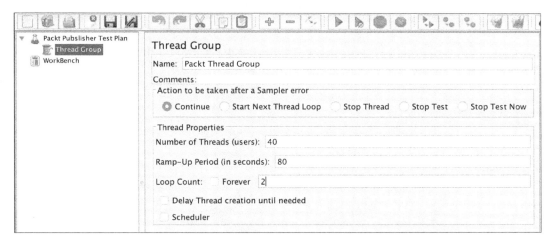

The thread group has the following important properties:

- **Number of Threads**: This is the number of virtual users.
- **The Ramp-Up period**: This tells JMeter how long it should take to ramp up to the full capacity of the number of threads. For example, in the preceding screenshot, we have 40 threads and 80 seconds of ramp-up time; here, JMeter will take 80 seconds to completely fire up 40 threads, and it will take 2 seconds for each of the three to start.

- **Loop Count**: This tells JMeter how much time it should take to run this thread group.

- **Scheduler**: This is used to schedule the execution of the thread group for a later time.

Now, we will need to add the HTTP request defaults. Right-click on **Packt Thread Group** and then go to **Add | Config Element | HTTP Request Defaults**. A window similar to the following will appear:

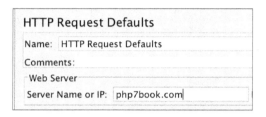

In the preceding window, we have to just enter the URL of the application or the IP address. If the web server uses cookies, we can add HTTP Cookie Manager too, in which we can add user-defined cookies with all the data, such as the name, value, domain, path, and so on.

Next, we will add an HTTP request by right-clicking and navigating to **Packt Thread Group | Add | Sampler | HTTP Request**, and the following window will appear:

The important field here is **Path**. We want to run the test only against the home page, so for this HTTP request, we will just add a slash (/) in the **Path** field. If we want to test another path, such as "Contact us", we will need to add another HTTP request sampler, as in the preceding screenshot. Then, in the path, we will add `path/contact-us`.

The HTTP Request sampler can be used to test forms too, where POST requests can be sent to the URL by selecting the POST method in the **Method** field. Also, file upload can be simulated.

The next step is to add some listeners. *Listeners provide some powerful views to display results.* The results can be displayed in a table view and different kinds of graphs can be saved in a file. For this thread group, we will add three listeners: View Results in Table, Response Time Graph, and Graph Results. Each listener view displays a different kind of data. Add all the preceding listeners by right-clicking on **Packt Thread Group** and then navigating to **Add | Listeners**. We will have a complete list of all the available listeners. Add all the three listeners one by one. Our final **Packt Publisher Test Plan** panel on the left-hand side of JMeter will look similar to the following:

Now, we are ready to run our test plan by clicking on the **Start** button in the upper tool bar, as shown in the following screenshot:

As soon as we click on the **Start** button (the green arrow pointing to the right-hand side), JMeter will start our test plan. Now, if we click on the **View Results in Table** listener on the left panel, we will see data for each request in a table, as shown in the following screenshot:

Sample #	Start Time	Thread Name	Label	Sample Time(ms)	Status	Bytes	Latency	Connect Time(ms)
8184	11:54:26.715	Packt Thread G...	HTTP Request	1754		64915	275	0
8185	11:54:27.504	Packt Thread G...	HTTP Request	1002		64915	276	0
8186	11:54:27.504	Packt Thread G...	HTTP Request	1004		64915	277	0
8187	11:54:27.412	Packt Thread G...	HTTP Request	1109		64915	288	0
8188	11:54:27.228	Packt Thread G...	HTTP Request	1307		64915	285	0
8189	11:54:27.574	Packt Thread G...	HTTP Request	1038		64915	320	0
8190	11:54:27.661	Packt Thread G...	HTTP Request	988		64915	268	0
8191	11:54:28.016	Packt Thread G...	HTTP Request	849		64915	285	0
8192	11:54:27.890	Packt Thread G...	HTTP Request	993		64915	291	0
8193	11:54:27.900	Packt Thread G...	HTTP Request	1030		64915	287	0
8194	11:54:27.653	Packt Thread G...	HTTP Request	1277		64915	271	0
8195	11:54:28.016	Packt Thread G...	HTTP Request	934		64915	282	0
8196	11:54:28.170	Packt Thread G...	HTTP Request	825		64915	280	0
8197	11:54:28.181	Packt Thread G...	HTTP Request	839		64915	279	0
8198	11:54:28.451	Packt Thread G...	HTTP Request	651		64915	275	0
8199	11:54:28.099	Packt Thread G...	HTTP Request	1105		64915	284	0
8200	11:54:28.192	Packt Thread G...	HTTP Request	1098		64915	282	0
8201	11:54:28.366	Packt Thread G...	HTTP Request	943		64915	303	0
8202	11:54:28.536	Packt Thread G...	HTTP Request	852		64915	273	0
8203	11:54:28.472	Packt Thread G...	HTTP Request	919		64915	259	0
8204	11:54:28.867	Packt Thread G...	HTTP Request	723		64915	274	0
8205	11:54:28.932	Packt Thread G...	HTTP Request	1000		64915	289	0
8206	11:54:29.311	Packt Thread G...	HTTP Request	744		64915	295	0
8207	11:54:29.292	Packt Thread G...	HTTP Request	942		64915	310	0
8208	11:54:29.592	Packt Thread G...	HTTP Request	765		64915	310	0
8209	11:54:29.934	Packt Thread G...	HTTP Request	837		64915	287	0

The preceding screenshot shows some interesting data, such as sample time, status, bytes, and latency.

Sample time is the number of milliseconds in which the server served the complete request. **Status** is the status of the request. It can be either a success, warning, or error. **Bytes** is the number of bytes received for the request. **Latency** is the number of milliseconds in which JMeter received the initial response from the server.

Now, if we click on **Response Time Graph**, we will see a visual graph for the response time, which is similar to the one that follows:

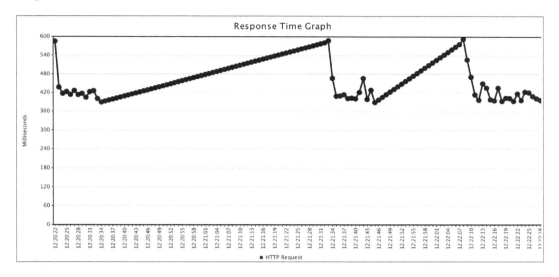

Now, if we click on **Graph Results**, we will see the response time data along with graphs for average, median, deviation, and throughput graphs, as shown in the following graph:

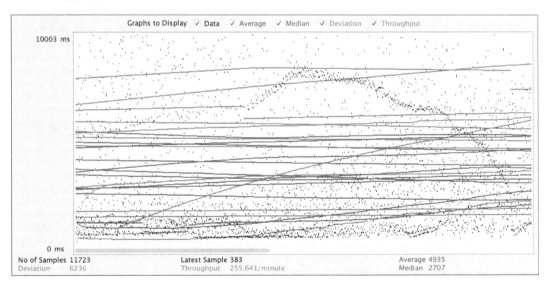

Apache JMeter provides very powerful tools to load test our web servers by simulating users. It can provide us with data regarding the amount of load that makes our web server's response slow, and using this data, we can optimize our web server and application.

ApacheBench (ab)

ApacheBench (ab) is also provided by Apache and is a command-line tool. It is a lovely tool for command line lovers. This tool is normally installed on most Linux flavors by default. Also, it is installed with Apache, so if you have Apache installed, you will probably have ab installed too.

The basic syntax for an ab command is as follows:

```
ab -n <Number_Requests> -c <Concurrency> <Address>:<Port><Path>
```

Let's discuss what each part of the preceding command means:

- n: This is the number of requests for test.
- c: This is concurrency, which is the number of simultaneous requests at a time.
- Address: This is either the application URL or IP address of the web server.
- Port: This is the port number at which the application is running.
- Path: This is the web path of the application that we can use to test. A slash (/) is used for the home page.

Now, let's conduct a test using the ab tool by issuing the following command:

```
ab -n 500 -c 10 packtpub.com/
```

As the default port for the web server is 80, it is not required to mention it. Note the slash at the end; this is required to place it there because it is the path's part.

After executing the preceding command, we will have an output that looks similar to the following:

```
Document Path:          /
Document Length:        0 bytes

Concurrency Level:      10
Time taken for tests:   1.020 seconds
Complete requests:      500
Failed requests:        0
Write errors:           0
Non-2xx responses:      500
Total transferred:      109000 bytes
HTML transferred:       0 bytes
Requests per second:    490.30 [#/sec] (mean)
Time per request:       20.396 [ms] (mean)
Time per request:       2.040 [ms] (mean, across all concurrent
Transfer rate:          104.38 [Kbytes/sec] received

Connection Times (ms)
              min  mean[+/-sd] median   max
Connect:       10   10   0.1     10      12
Processing:    10   10   2.2     10      43
Waiting:       10   10   2.2     10      43
Total:         19   20   2.2     20      52

Percentage of the requests served within a certain time (ms)
  50%     20
  66%     20
  75%     20
  80%     20
  90%     20
  95%     20
  98%     22
  99%     28
 100%     52 (longest request)
----------------------------------------------------------------
~ #
```

We can see some useful information here, including the number of requests per second, which is **490.3**; the total time taken for the test, which is **1.020 seconds**; the shortest request, which is **20 ms**; and the longest request, which is **52 ms**.

The server load limit can be found by increasing the number of requests and concurrency level and checking the web server's performance.

Siege

Siege is another command-line open source tool to test load and performance. Siege is an HTTP/FTP load tester and benchmarking utility. It is designed for developers and administrators to measure the performance of their applications under load. It can send a configurable number of simultaneous requests to a server and those requests that place the server under a siege.

Its installation is simple and easy. For Linux and Mac OS X, first download Siege by issuing the following command in the terminal:

```
wget http://download.joedog.org/siege/siege-3.1.4.tar.gz
```

It will download the Siege TAR compressed file. Now, uncompress it by issuing the following command:

```
tar -xvf siege-3.1.4.tar.gz
```

Now, all the files will be in the `siege-3.1.4` folder. Build and install it by issuing the following commands one by one in the terminal:

```
cd siege-3.1.4
./configure
make
make install
```

Now, Siege is installed. To confirm this, issue the following command to check the Siege version:

```
siege -V
```

If it displays the version with some other information, then Siege is installed successfully.

 As of writing this book, the current Siege stable version is 3.1.4. Also, Siege does not support Windows natively, and, of course, Windows servers can be tested and benchmarked using Siege.

Now, let's have a load test. A basic load test can be executed by running the following command:

```
siege some_url_or_ip
```

Siege will then start the test. We have to enter the application URL or server IP that we want to load test. To stop the test, press *Ctrl + C*, and we will have an output similar to the following:

```
HTTP/1.1 200   0.39 secs:    13034 bytes ==> GET  /
HTTP/1.1 200   0.49 secs:    13034 bytes ==> GET  /
^C
Lifting the server siege..        done.

Transactions:                   223 hits
Availability:                100.00 %
Elapsed time:                 14.52 secs
Data transferred:              2.77 MB
Response time:                 0.40 secs
Transaction rate:             15.36 trans/sec
Throughput:                    0.19 MB/sec
Concurrency:                   6.18
Successful transactions:        223
Failed transactions:             0
Longest transaction:           1.22
Shortest transaction:          0.36

LOG FILE: /usr/local/var/siege.log
```

In the preceding screenshot we can see **Transactions**, **Response time**, and **Transaction rate** along with **Longest transaction** and **Shortest transaction**.

By default, Siege creates 15 concurrent users. This can be changed by using the -c option, which is done by making the following alteration in the command:

```
siege url_or_ip -c 100
```

However, Siege has a limitation for the concurrent users, which may be different for each OS. This can be set in the Siege configuration file. To find out the config file location and concurrent user limit, issue the following command in terminal:

```
siege -C
```

A list of the configuration options will be displayed. Also the resource file or config file location will be displayed. Open that file and find the config concurrent and set its value to an appropriate required value.

Another important feature of Siege is that a file that has all the URLs that need to be tested can be used. The file should have a single URL in each line. The -f flag is used with Siege as follows:

```
siege -f /path/to/url/file.txt -c 120
```

Siege will load the file and start load testing each URL.

Another interesting feature of Siege is the internet mode, which can be entered using the -i flag in the following command:

```
siege -if path_to_urls_file -c 120
```

In the internet mode, each URL is hit randomly and mimics a real-life situation, in which it can't be predicted which URL will be hit.

> Siege has lots of useful flags and features. A detailed list can be found in the official documentation at https://www.joedog.org/siege-manual/.

Load testing real-world applications

We studied three tools in this chapter to load test. Now, it is time to load test some real-world applications. In this section, we will test Magento 2, Drupal 8, and WordPress 4. All these open source tools will have their default data.

We have three VPS configured with NGINX as the web server. One VPS has PHP 5.5-FPM, the second has PHP 5.6-FPM, and the third has PHP 7-FPM installed. The hardware specs for all the three VPS are same, and all applications we will test will have the same data and the same versions.

This way, we will benchmark these applications with PHP 5.5, PHP 5.6, and PHP 7 and take a look at how fast these applications can run on different versions of PHP.

> In this topic, we won't cover configuring the servers with NGINX, PHP, and the databases. We will assume that the VPS are configured and that Magento 2, Drupal 8, and WordPress 4 are installed on them.

Magento 2

Magento 2 is installed on all VPS, and all the caches are enabled for Magento. PHP OPcache is also enabled. After running the tests, we got an average result for all the three Magento 2 installations, as shown in the following graphs:

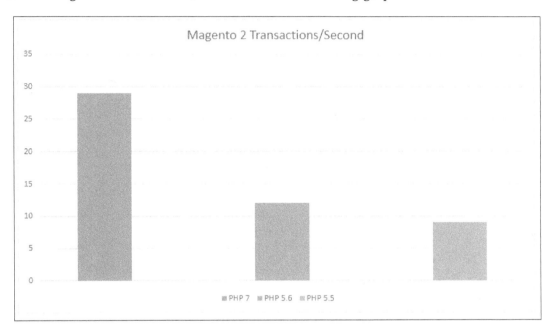

In the preceding chart, the vertical line, or Y-axis, shows the transactions per second. As can be seen in the charts, Magento 2 on PHP 7 has 29 transactions per second, while the same Magento 2 installation on the same hardware with PHP 5.6 has 12 transactions per second. Also, on PHP 5.5, the same Magento installation has 9 transactions per second. So, in this case, Magento runs about 241% faster on PHP 7 than PHP 5.6 and about 320% faster than in PHP 5.5. This is a very huge improvement of PHP 7 on both PHP 5.6 and PHP 5.5.

WordPress 4

WordPress is installed on all of the three VPS. Unfortunately, there is no default cache embedded into WordPress, and we will not install any third-party modules, so no cache is used. The results are still good, as can be seen in the following graphs. PHP OPcache is enabled.

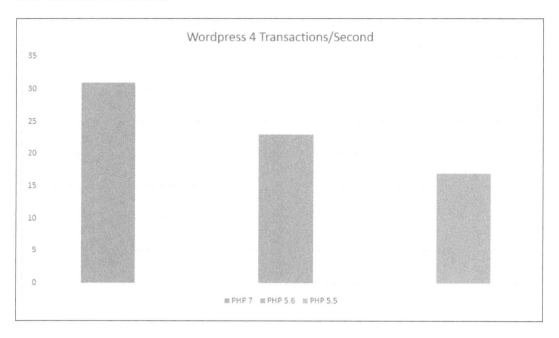

As can be seen in the preceding graph, WordPress runs 135% faster in PHP 7 than in PHP 5.6 and 182% faster than in PHP 5.5.

Drupal 8

We used the same VPS for PHP 5.5, PHP 5.6, and PHP 7. The default Drupal 8 cache is enabled. After load testing the default home of Drupal 8, we got the following results:

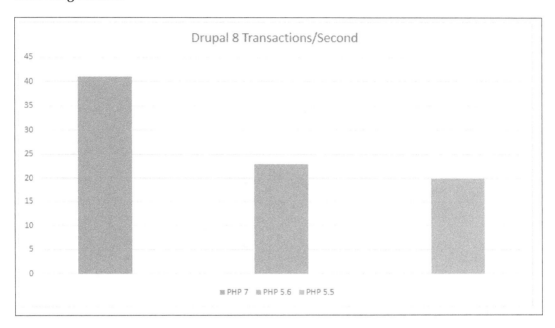

The preceding graph shows that Drupal 8 runs 178% faster in PHP 7 than in PHP 5.6 and 205% faster than in PHP 5.5.

In the preceding graphs, all these values are approximate values. If a low-power hardware is used, then smaller values will be generated. If we use a more powerful multiprocessor-dedicated server with the web server and database optimizations, we will get higher values. The point to consider is that we will always get better performance for PHP 7 than PHP 5.6.

A combined graph is shown here, which displays the performance improvements for different applications in PHP 7 over PHP 5.5 and PHP 5.6:

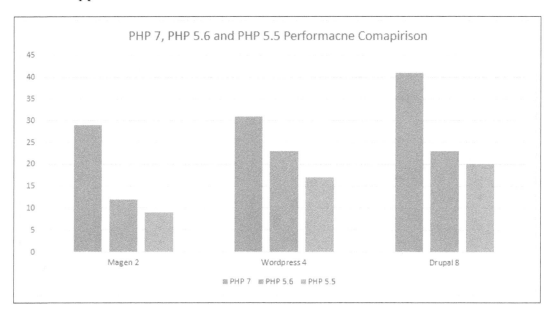

Summary

In this chapter, we discussed a few load testing and benchmarking tools, such as JMeter, ApacheBench (ab), and Siege. We used each tool to load test, and discussed the output and what it means. Finally, we load tested three famous open source applications, Magento 2, WordPress 4, and Drupal 8, and created graphs for each application's transactions per second in both PHP 7 and PHP 5.6.

In the next chapter, we will discuss best practices for PHP development. These practices are not limited only to PHP and can be used for any programming language.

7
Best Practices in PHP Programming

So far, we discussed performance-related topics. Now, in this chapter, we will study best practices in PHP applications' development and deployment. This is a vast topic, but we will cover it briefly. PHP provides all levels of programmers with the ability to write quality code easily and quickly. However, when the application advances to a more complex nature, we forget to follow the best practices. To produce a high performance PHP application, it is necessary to keep in mind the performance at every line of the code.

We will cover the following topics:

- Coding styles
- Design patterns
- Service-oriented architecture (SOA)
- Test-driven development (TDD) and PHPUnit testing
- PHP frameworks
- Version control systems and Git
- Deployment

Coding styles

There are too many coding styles out there, such as PSR-0, PSR-1, PSR-2, PSR-3, and so on. Programmers can use different standards as they want, but it is necessary to follow a standard that is already used in the libraries or a framework in use to make the code more readable. For example, Laravel uses the PSR-1 and PSR-4 coding standards, so if we are developing in Laravel, we should follow these coding standards. Some PHP frameworks, such as Yii 2 and **Zend Framework 2**, follow the PSR-2 coding standards. However, none of these frameworks stick to a single standard; most of them follow a mixed standard according to their requirements.

The important point is to follow the standard that is used in the libraries used in the application. An organization can also use its own coding standards for internal purposes. It is not a requirement for coding; it is a requirement for readability and producing quality code that others can understand.

PHP Framework Interop Group (PHP-FIG) is a group whose members defined coding standards for PHP. Full details about PSR standards can be found on their website at `http://www.php-fig.org/`.

Instead of discussing a specific coding standard, let's discuss best practices in coding styles for PHP:

- The first letter of each word in the class name must be capital. The opening brace should be on the line after the class declaration, and the closing brace should be on the line after the class end line. Here's an example:

```
class Foo
{
    ...
    ...
    ...
}
```

- Class methods and function names should follow the camel case naming convention. The starting braces should be on the next line of the class declaration, and the end brace should be on the line at the end of the function definition. There should be no spaces between the method name and the parenthesis. Also, there should be no space between the first argument, the opening parenthesis, the last argument, and the closing parenthesis. Also, there should be no space between an argument and the comma at the end of this argument, but there should be a space between a comma and the next argument. Here's an example:

```
public function phpBook($arg1, $arg2, $arg3)
{
```

```
    ...
    ...
    ...
}
```

- If there is a namespace declaration, there must be a single empty line after its declaration. If there are use declarations, all of them must go after that namespace's declarations. There must be one use declaration per line, and there must be a space after the use block. Also, the `extends` and `implements` keywords must be on the same line as the class declaration. Here's an example:

```
namespace Packt\Videos;

use Packt\Books;
use Packt\Presentations;

class PacktClass extends VideosClass implements BaseClass
{
    ...
    ...
    ...
}
```

- Visibility must be declared for all properties, and the properties must be in camel case. Also, properties must not be prepended with an underscore for private or protected visibilities. Take a look at the following example:

```
class PacktClass
{
    public $books;
    private $electronicBooks;
    ...
    ...
    ...
}
```

- If there is an `abstract` keyword, it must come before the `class` keyword for classes, and the `final` keyword must come before the method's visibility in the case of methods. On the other hand, the `static` keyword must come after the method visibility. Take a look at this example:

```
abstract class PacktClass
{
    final public static function favoriteBooks()
    {
        ...
```

```
   ...
     ...
   }
 }
```

- All PHP keywords must be used in lowercase, including the `true` and `false` keywords. Constants must be declared and used in capital case.

- For all control structures, there must be a space after the control structure keyword. If there is an expression for this control structure, there must be no space between the parenthesis holding this expression and the block of code that follows. There must be a space after the parenthesis and the starting brace. The starting brace must be on the same line as the control structure. The closing brace must be on the line after the end of the body. Refer to the following code for a better understanding:

```
if ($book == "PHP 7") {
  ...
  ...
  ...
} else {
  ...
  ...
  ...
}
```

- In the case of loops, the spaces must be as in the following examples:

```
for ($h = 0; $h < 10; $h++) {
  ...
  ...
  ...
}

foreach ($books as $key => $value) {
  ...
  ...
  ...
}

while ($book) {
  ...
  ...
  ...
}
```

For the purpose of this book, I did not follow the rule of the opening brace being on the same line as the control structure declaration and always used it on the next line of the declaration. I did not find it clearer; it is a personal choice, and anybody can follow the standards mentioned here.

Standards are good to follow as they make the code more readable and professional. However, never try to invent your own new standards; always follow those that are already invented and followed by the community.

Test-driven development (TDD)

Test-driven development is the process of testing every aspect of the application during development. Either the tests are defined before development and then development is made to pass these tests, or the classes and libraries are built and then tested. Testing the application is very important, and launching an application without tests is like jumping from a 30-floor-high building without a parachute.

PHP does not provide any built-in features to test, but there are other test frameworks that can be used for this purpose. One of most widely used frameworks or libraries is PHPUnit. It is a very powerful tool and provides lots of features. Now, let's have a look at it.

The installation of PHPUnit is easy. Just download it and place it in your project root so that it can be accessed from the command line.

 PHPUnit installation and basic details, including features and examples, can be found at https://phpunit.de/.

Let's have a simple example. We have a Book class, as follows:

```
class Book
{
  public $title;
  public function __construct($title)
  {
    $this->title = $title;
  }

  public function getBook()
  {
    return $this->title;
  }
}
```

This is an example of a simple class that initializes the `title` property when the class is instantiated. When the `getBook` method is called, it returns the title of the book.

Now, we want to make a test in which we will check whether the `getBook` method returns `PHP 7` as a title. So, perform the following steps to create the test:

1. Create a `tests` directory at your project's root. Create a `BookTest.php` file in the `tests` directory.

2. Now, place the following code in the `BookTest.php` file:

    ```php
    include (__DIR__.'/../Book.php');

    class BookTest extends PHPUnit_Framework_TestCase
    {
      public function testBookClass()
      {
        $expected = 'PHP 7';
        $book = new Book('PHP 7');
        $actual = $book->getBook();
        $this->assertEquals($expected, $book);
      }
    }
    ```

3. Now, we have written our first test. Note that we named our class `BookTest`, which extends the `PHPUnit_Framework_TestCase` class. We can name our test class whatever we want. However, the name should be easily recognizable so that we know this is written for the class that needs to be tested.

4. Then, we added a method named `testBookClass`. We are also free to select whatever name we want to give to this method, but it should start with the word `test`. If not, PHPUnit will not execute the method and will issue a warning — in our case, for the preceding test class — that no tests were found.

    In the `testBookClass` method, we created an object of the `Book` class and passed `PHP 7` as our title. Then, we fetched the title using the `getBook` method of the `Book` class. The important part is the last line of the `testBookClass` method, which performs the assertion and checks whether the data returned from `getBook` is the desired data or not.

5. Now, we are ready to run our first test. Open the command line or terminal in the root of the project and issue the following command:

    ```
    php phpunit.phar tests/BookTest.php
    ```

When the command is executed, we will have an output similar to the following screenshot:

```
/Applications/XAMPP/xamppfiles/htdocs/tests/php7/phpunit » php phpunit.phar tests/BookTest.php
PHPUnit 5.2.11 by Sebastian Bergmann and contributors.

.                                                                          1 / 1 (100%)

Time: 62 ms, Memory: 10.50Mb

OK (1 test, 1 assertion)
```

Our test is executed successfully as it met the criteria defined in our test.

6. Now, let's change our class a little bit and pass PHP to the Book class, as shown in the following code:

```
public function testBookClass()
{
    $book = new Book('PHP');
    $title = $book->getBook();
    $this->assertEquals('PHP 7', $book);
}
```

7. Now, we are looking for PHP 7, and our Book class returns PHP, so it does not pass our test. After executing this test, we will have a failure, as shown in the following screenshot:

```
/Applications/XAMPP/xamppfiles/htdocs/tests/php7/phpunit » php phpunit.phar tests/BookTest.php
PHPUnit 5.2.11 by Sebastian Bergmann and contributors.

F                                                                          1 / 1 (100%)

Time: 65 ms, Memory: 10.50Mb

There was 1 failure:

1) BookTest::testBookClass
Failed asserting that two strings are equal.
--- Expected
+++ Actual
@@ @@
-'PHP 7'
+'PHP'

/Applications/XAMPP/xamppfiles/htdocs/tests/php7/phpunit/tests/BookTest.php:12

FAILURES!
Tests: 1, Assertions: 1, Failures: 1.
```

As seen in the preceding screenshot, we expected PHP 7, and we got an actual result of PHP 7. The – sign shows the expected value, and the + sign shows the actual value.

 In the previous topic, we discussed how we can perform tests on our libraries. We only discussed a simple basic test. PHPUnit is not limited to these simple tests, but covering PHPUnit completely is out of the scope of this book. A very nice book on PHPUnit is *PHPUnit Essentials*, published by Packt Publishing.

Design patterns

A design pattern solves a specific problem. It is not a tool; it is just a description or template that describes how to solve a specific problem. Design patterns are important, and they play a good role in writing clean and clear code.

One of the most widely used design patterns in the PHP community is the **Model View Controller** (**MVC**) pattern. Most PHP frameworks are built upon this pattern. MVC advises you to keep the business logic and data operations (that is, the model) separate from the presentation (the view). Controllers just play the role of a middleman between models and views and make the communication between them possible. There is no direct communication between models and views. If a view needs any kind of data, it sends a request to the controller. The controller knows how to operate on this request and, if needed, make a call to the model to perform any operation on the data (fetch, insert, validate, delete, and so on). Then at last, the controller sends a response to the view.

In best practices, fat models and skinny controllers are used. This means that controllers are only used to take a specific action on a request and nothing else. Even in some modern frameworks, the validation is moved out of the controllers and is performed at the model level. These models perform all the operations on the data. In modern frameworks, models are considered as a layer, which can have multiple parts, such as the business logic, **Create Read Update Delete** (**CRUD**) database operations, data mapper pattern and services, and so on. So, a full load of models and controllers is just sitting there and enjoying the lazy work load.

Another widely used design pattern is the factory design pattern. This pattern simply creates objects that are needed to be used. Another good pattern is the observer pattern, in which an object calls different observers on a specific event or task on it. This is mainly used for event handling. Yet another widely used pattern is the **singleton pattern**, which is used when there is a requirement that only a single object of a class be used throughout the application's execution. *A singleton object can't be serialized and cloned.*

Service-oriented architecture (SOA)

In service-oriented architecture, the application's components provide services to each other on a defined protocol. Each component is loosely coupled with each other, and the only way of communication between them is through the services they provide.

In PHP, Symfony provides the best way to have SOA as it is mainly an HTTP-centric framework. Symfony is the most mature, well-tested collection of libraries that are widely used by other PHP frameworks, such as Zend Framework, Yii, Laravel, and others.

Let's consider a scenario where we have a backend and a frontend for a website and a mobile application. Normally, in most applications, the backend and frontend run on the same code base and on a single access point, and an API or web service is built for mobile applications to communicate with this backend. It is good, but we need great. So, for high performance and scalable applications, the separate components run independently of each other. If they need to communicate with each other, they communicate through the web services.

Web services are the central communication point between the frontend and backend and between the backend and mobile applications. The backend is the main hub of data and any other business logic. It can be standalone and built using any programming language, such as PHP. The frontend can be built using normal HTML/CSS, AngularJS, Node.js, jQuery, or any other technology for the frontend. Similarly, mobile apps can be native or built on cross-platform technologies. The backend doesn't care what the frontend and mobile apps are built on.

Being object-oriented and reusable always

This may seem difficult for a small, single-page application in which only a few things are happening, but this is not the case. The classes are easy to handle, and the code is always clear. Also, the classes separate the application logic from the views. This make things more logical. In the earlier days when structure code was used and a bunch of functions had to be created either in the view files or in a separate file, this would have been too easy. However, when applications got more complex, it got more difficult to handle.

Always try to create loosely coupled classes to make them more reusable in other applications. Also, always perform a single task in each method of the class.

PHP frameworks

We all know about frameworks, and they are not essential to a programmer's life. There are lots of frameworks, and each framework has its own superiority over other frameworks in some features. All frameworks are good, but what make a framework not suitable for an application are the application's requirements.

Let's say that we want to build an enterprise-level CRM application, which framework will suit us best? This is the most important, confusing, and time-wasting question. First, we need to know the complete requirements for the CRM application, usage capacity, features, data security, and performance.

Version control system (VCS) and Git

Version controller system provides the flexibility to properly maintain code, changes, and versions of the application. Using VCS, a complete team can work together on an application, and they can pull other team members' changes and their own changes to the system without any big troubles. In case of a disaster, VCS provides the ability to fall back to an old, more stable version of the application.

Oh wait! Are we talking about VCS? Did we mention Git? Nope! So, let's start with Git.

Git is a powerful tool. It monitors changes in each file in a branch, and when pushed to a remote branch, only the changed files are uploaded. Git keeps a history of the file changes and provides you with the ability to compare the changed files.

 A very informative and good book on Git is *Git Essentials* published by Packt Publishing. Also, an official and free book about Git can be found at https://git-scm.com/book/en/v2.

Deployment and Continuous Integration (CI)

FTP is obsolete. It is not feasible for today, it makes things slow, and a normal FTP connection is insecure. It is hard for a team to deploy their changes using FTP because it creates huge conflicts in their code and this may cause problems, while uploading changes and can override each other's changes.

Using a Git versioning system, such as GitHub, GitLab, and Bitbucket, we can make our deployment automatic. Different developers use different setups for automatic deployments, and it all depends on their own choice and ease. The general rules of using automatic deployments are to make them easy for a team and to not use FTP.

The following is a general flowchart for a deployment setup:

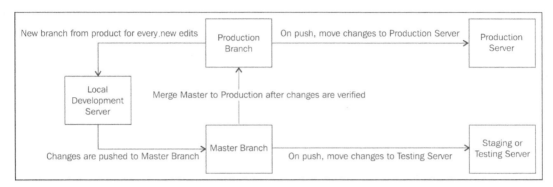

As shown in the preceding flowchart, we have two servers: the staging or testing the server and production server. On the staging server, we have an exact copy of the website to test new features and others, and the production server has our live website.

Now, we have a repository that has two main branches: the master branch and the production branch. The master branch is used for development and testing purposes, and the production branch is used for final production features. Note that the production branch should only accept merging, and it should not accept commits so that the production environment is completely safe.

Now, let's say that we want to add a customer registration feature to our application. We will perform the following steps:

1. The first and most important thing to do is to create a new branch from the production branch head. Let's name this branch customer-registration.

2. Now, add all the new features to this customer-registration branch and while verifying on the local development server, merge this branch to the local master branch.

3. After merging the new branch to the local master branch, push the master branch to remote master branch. A successful push will cause the new features to be moved to the staging server.

4. Now, test all the new features on the staging server.

5. When everything works fine, merge the remote master branch with the remote production branch. This will cause all the changes to be moved to the production branch, and this merge will cause all the new changes to be moved to the production server.

6. An ideal setup similar to the preceding one makes deployment very easy, and a complete team can work on the application regardless of the geographical location. In case any issue occurs during the deployment, one can be easily fall back to the old version of the production branch.

Continuous Integration (**CI**) is a technique in which all the members of a team have to integrate their code into a shared repository, and then each check by the team member is verified by automatic builds to catch errors and problems in the early stages.

There are several tools that are used for CI for PHP; some of these are PHPCI, Jenkins, Travis CI, and others.

Summary

In this chapter, we discussed a few best practices, including coding standards and styles, PHP frameworks, design patterns, Git, and deployment. Also, we discussed the PHPUnit framework to test classes and libraries against tests. Also, we discussed Service-oriented design, which plays a major role in creating APIs for applications.

In this book, we studied setting up development environments, including Linux servers, specifically Debian and Ubuntu, and we also discussed Vagrant. The new features of PHP are also listed with sample codes. You read in detail about the tools that we can use to improve the performance of an application and a database. Also, we discussed debugging and stress or load testing our applications and some best practices of writing quality code.

We mostly summarized the tools and techniques with simple examples to introduce the reader to these tools and techniques. There is a good chance that each tool and technique has its own book written for a more advanced usage. We recommend you follow up on these tools and techniques and conduct more research for their advance usage. Good luck Php-ing!

A
Tools to Make Life Easy

We covered many things in this book, starting with new features in PHP 7 and ending with the best techniques in programming. In each chapter, we used and talked about some tools, but due to the finite length of chapters and the book, we did not go too much in detail for these tools. In this appendix, we will discuss three of these tools in much more detail. The tools we will to discuss are as follows:

- Composer
- Git
- Grunt watch

So, let's start.

Composer – A dependency manager for PHP

Composer is a dependency management tool for PHP that enables us to define dependencies for a PHP application, and Composer installs/updates them. Composer is completely written in PHP and is an application in the PHP Archive (PHAR) format.

 Composer downloads dependencies from https://packagist. org/. Any dependency for an application can be installed through Composer as long as it is available on Packagist. Also, complete applications can be installed through Composer if they are available at Packagist.

Composer installation

Composer is a command line tool and can be installed globally in the operating system, or the `composer.phar` file can be placed in the root of the application and then executed from the command line. For Windows, an executable setup file is provided, which can be used to install Composer globally. For this book, we will follow the instructions for Debian/Ubuntu globally. Perform the following steps:

1. Issue the following command to download the Composer installer. The file name is `installer` and can only be executed with PHP once installed via the following code:

   `Wget https://getcomposer.org/installer`

2. Issue the following command to install it globally on Debian or Ubuntu:

   `Php install --install-dir=/usr/local/bin --filename=composer`

   This command will download Composer and will install it in the `/usr/local/bin` directory with the file name `composer`. Now, we will be able to run Composer globally.

3. Verify the Composer installation by issuing the following command in the terminal:

   `Composer --version`

   If the Composer version is displayed, then Composer is successfully installed globally.

 If Composer is installed locally to an application, then we will have a `composer.phar` file. The commands are the same, but all the commands should be executed with PHP. For example, `php composer.phar --version` will display the Composer version.

Now, Composer is installed successfully and is working; it's time to use it.

Using Composer

To use Composer in our project, we will need a `composer.json` file. This file contains all the dependencies required for the project and some other metadata. Composer uses this file to install and update different libraries.

Let's assume that our application needs to log different information in different ways. For this, we can use the `monolog` library. First, we will create a `composer.json` file in the root of our application and add the following code to it:

```
{
    "require": {
        "monolog/monolog": "1.0.*"
    }
}
```

After saving the file, execute the following command to install the dependencies of the application:

```
Composer install
```

This command will download the dependencies and place them in the `vendor` directory, as can be seen in the following screenshot:

```
Loading composer repositories with package information
Updating dependencies (including require-dev)
  - Installing monolog/monolog (1.0.2)
    Downloading: 100%

Writing lock file
Generating autoload files
→ packt ls
composer.json  composer.lock  vendor
→ packt |
```

As can be seen in the preceding screenshot, monolog version 1.0.2 is downloaded, and a `vendor` directory is created. The `monolog` library is placed in this directory. Also, if a package has to autoload information, then Composer places the library in the Composer autoloader, which is also placed in the `vendor` directory. So, any new libraries or dependencies will be autoloaded automatically during the application's execution.

Also a new file can be seen, which is `composer.lock`. When Composer downloads and installs any dependencies, the exact version and other information is written to this file to lock the application to this specific version of dependencies. This ensures that all the team members or whoever wants to set up the application will use the exact same version of the dependencies, and thus, it will reduce the chances of using different versions of dependencies.

Nowadays, Composer is widely used for package management. Big open source projects such as Magento, Zend Framework, Laravel, Yii, and many others are easily available for installation through Composer. We will install some of these in the next appendix using Composer.

Git – A version control system

Git is the most widely used version control system. According to the Git official website, it is a distributed version control system capable of handling everything from small- to large-sized projects with speed and efficiency.

Git installation

Git is available for all major operating systems. For Windows, an executable setup file is provided that can be used to install Git and use it in the command line. On OS X, Git comes already installed, but if it is not found, it can be downloaded from their official website. To install Git on Debian/Ubuntu, just issue the following command in the terminal:

```
sudo apt-get install git
```

After installation, issue the following command to check whether it is properly installed:

```
git -version
```

Then, we will see the current installed version of Git.

Using Git

For a better understanding of Git, we will start with a test project. Our test project name is `packt-git`. For this project, we also created a GitHub repository named `packt-git`, where will push our project files.

First, we will initialize Git in our project by issuing the following command:

```
git init
```

The preceding command will initialize an empty Git repository in our project root directory, and the head will be kept on the master branch, which is the default branch for every Git repository. It will create a hidden `.git` directory that will contain all the information about the repository. Next, we will add a remote repository that we will create on GitHub. I created a test repository at GitHub that has the URL `https://github.com/altafhussain10/packt-git.git`.

Now, issue the following command to add the GitHub repository to our empty repository:

```
git remote add origion https://github.com/altafhussain10/packt-git.git
```

Now, create a README.md file at your project root and add some content to it. The README.md file is used to display the repository information and other details about the repository at Git. This file is also used to display instructions regarding how to use the repository and/or the project for which this repository is created.

Now, issue the following command to see the status of our Git repository:

```
git status
```

This command will display the status of the repository, as can be seen in the following screenshot:

```
~/packt-git(branch:master*) » git status
On branch master

Initial commit

Untracked files:
  (use "git add <file>..." to include in what will be committed)

        README.md

nothing added to commit but untracked files present (use "git add" to track)
```

As can be seen in the preceding screenshot, we have an untracked file in our repository that is not committed yet. First, we will add the files to be tracked by issuing the following command in the terminal:

```
git add README.md
```

The git add command updates the index using the current contents found in the working tree. This command adds all the changes made to the path. There are some options that can be used to add some specific changes. The previous command we used will only add the README.md file to the track in the repository. So, if we want to track all the files, then we will use the following command:

```
git add
```

This will start tracking all the files in the current working directory or at the root of the current branch. Now, if we want to track some specific files, such as all files with the `.php` extension, then we can use it as follows:

```
git add '*.php
```

This will add all the files with the `.php` extension to track.

Next, we will commit changes or additions to our repository using the following command:

```
git commit -m "Initial Commit"
```

The `git commit` command commits all the changes to the local repository. The `-m` flag specifies any log message to `commit`. Remember that the changes are only committed to the local repository.

Now, we will push the changes to our remote repository using the following command:

```
git push -u origion master
```

The preceding command will push all the changes from the local repository to the remote repository or origin. The `-u` flag is used to set the upstream, and it links our local repo to our remote central repo. As we pushed our changes for the first time, we have to use the `-u` option. After this, we can just use the following command:

```
git push
```

This will push all the changes to the main repository of the current branch at which we are.

Creating new branches and merging

New branches are always required during development. If any kind of changes are required, it is good to create a new branch for these changes. Then, make all the changes on this branch and finally commit, merge, and push them to the remote origin.

To better understand this, let's suppose we want to fix an issue in the login page. The issue is about validation errors. We will name our new branch `login_validation_errors_fix`. It is good practice to give a more understandable name to branches. Also, we would like to create this new branch from the master branch head. This means that we want the new branch to inherit all the data from the master branch. So, if we are not at the master branch, we have to use the following command to switch to the master branch:

```
git checkout master
```

The preceding command will switch us to the master branch no matter which branch we are at. To create the branch, issue the following command in the terminal:

```
git branch login_validation_errors_fix
```

Now, our new branch is created from the master branch head, so all the changes should be made to this new branch. After all the changes and fixes are done, we have to commit the changes to the local and remote repositories. Note that we did not create the new branch in our remote repository. Now, let's commit the changes using the following command:

```
git commit -a -m "Login validation errors fix"
```

Note that we did not use git add to add the changes or new additions. To automatically commit our changes, we used the -a option in commit, which will add all the files automatically. If git add is used, then there is no need to use the -a option in commit. Now, our changes are committed to the local repository. We will need to push the changes to the remote origin. Issue the following command in the terminal:

```
git push -u origion login_validation_errors_fix
```

The preceding command will create a new branch at the remote repository, set the tracking of the same local branch to the remote branch, and push all the changes to it.

Now, we want to merge the changes with our master branch. First, we need to switch to our master branch using the following command:

```
git checkout master
```

Next, we will issue the following commands to merge our new branch login_validation_errors_fix with the master branch:

```
git checkout master
git merge login_validation_errors_fix
git push
```

It is important to switch to the branch to which we want to merge our new branch. After this, we need to use the git merge branch_to_merge syntax to merge this branch with the current branch. Finally, we can just push to the remote origin. Now, if we take a look at our remote repository, we will see the new branch and also the changes in our master branch.

Cloning a repository

Sometimes, we need to work on a project that is hosted on a repository. For this, we will first clone this repository, which will download the complete repository to our local system, and then create a local repository for this remote repository. The rest of the working is the same as we discussed before. To clone a repository, we should first know the remote repository web address. Let's say that we want to clone the PHPUnit repository. If we go to the GitHub repository for PHPUnit, we will see the web address of the repository at the upper right-hand side, as shown in the screenshot that follows:

The URL just after the **HTTPS** button is the web address for this repository. Copy this URL and use the following command to clone this repository:

```
git clone https://github.com/sebastianbergmann/phpunit.git
```

This will start downloading the repository. After it is completed, we will have a PHPUnit folder that will have the repository and all its files. Now, all the operations mentioned in the preceding topics can be performed.

Webhooks

One of the most powerful features of Git is webhooks. Webhooks are events that are fired when a specific action occurs on the repository. If an event or hook for the Push request is made, then this hook will be fired every time a push is made to this repository.

To add a webhook to a repository, click on the **Settings** link for the repository in the upper right-hand side. In the new page, on the left-hand side, we will have a **Webhooks and Services** link. Click on it, and we will see a page similar to the following one:

Webhooks / **Add webhook**

We'll send a POST request to the URL below with details of any subscribed events. You can also specify which data format you'd like to receive (JSON, x-www-form-urlencoded, *etc*). More information can be found in our developer documentation.

Payload URL *

```
https://packtphp7.com/git/hooks/push
```

Content type

```
application/json                    ⬍
```

Secret

```
```

🔒 By default, we verify SSL certificates when delivering payloads.   **Disable SSL verification**

Which events would you like to trigger this webhook?

◉ Just the push event.

○ Send me **everything.**

○ Let me select individual events.

☑ **Active**
   We will deliver event details when this hook is triggered.

Add webhook

As can be seen in the preceding screenshot, we have to enter a payload URL, which will be called every time our selected event is fired. In **Content type**, we will select the data format in which the payload will be sent to our URL. In the events section, we can select whether we want only push events or all the events; we can select multiple events for which we want this hook to be fired. After saving this hook, it will be fired every time the selected event occurs.

Webhooks are mostly used for deployment. When the changes are pushed and if there is a webhook for the push event, the specific URL is called. Then, this URL executes some command to download the changes and processes them on the local server and places them at the appropriate place. Also, webhooks are used for continues integration and to deploy to cloud services.

Desktop tools to manage repositories

There are several tools that can be used to manage Git repositories. GitHub provides its own tool called GitHub Desktop that can be used to manage GitHub repositories. This can be used to create new repositories, see the history, and push, pull, and clone repositories. It provides every feature that we can use in the command line. The screenshot that follows shows our test `packt-git` repository:

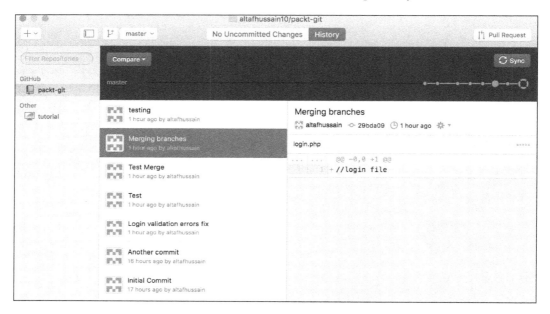

 GitHub Desktop can be downloaded from `https://desktop.github.com/` and is available for Mac and Windows only. Also, GitHub Desktop can be only used with GitHub unless some hacks are used to make it work with other repositories, such as GitLab or Bitbucket.

Another powerful tool is SourceTree. SourceTree can be used with GitHub, GitLab, and Bitbucket easily. It provides complete features to manage repositories, pull, push, commit, merge, and other actions. SourceTree provides a very powerful and beautiful graph tool for the branches and commits. The following is a screenshot for SourceTree that is used to connect with our `packt-git` test repository:

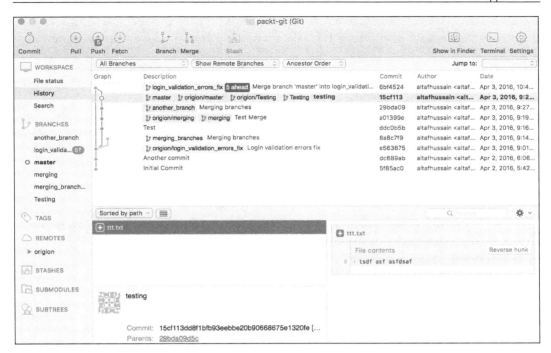

Besides the previous two nice tools, every development IDE provides version control systems with full support and also provides features such as different colors for modified and newly added files.

Git is a powerful tool; it can't be covered in this appendix. There are several books available, but Git Book is a very good place to start. This can be downloaded in different formats from `https://git-scm.com/book/en/v2` or can be read online.

Grunt watch

We studied Grunt in *Chapter 3, Improving PHP 7 Application Performance*. We only used it to merge CSS and JavaScript files and minify them. However, Grunt is not used only for this purpose. It is a JavaScript task runner, which can run tasks either by watching specific files for changes or by manually running tasks. We studied how we can run tasks manually, so now we will study how to use grunt watch to run specific tasks when some changes are made.

Grunt watch is useful and saves a lot of time because it runs the specific tasks automatically instead of running the tasks manually every time we change something.

Let's recall our examples from *Chapter 3, Improving PHP 7 Application Performance.* We used Grunt to combine and compress CSS and JavaScript files. For this purpose, we created four tasks. One task was combining all CSS files, the second task was combining all JavaScript files, the third task was compressing the CSS files, and the fourth task was compressing all JavaScript files. It will be very time consuming if we run all these tasks manually every time we make some changes. Grunt provides a feature called watch that watches different destinations for file changes, and if any change occurs, it executes the tasks that are defined in the watch.

First, check whether the `grunt watch` module is installed or not. Check the `node_modules` directory and see whether there is another directory with the name `grunt-contrib-watch`. If this directory is there, then watch is already installed. If the directory is not there, then just issue the following command in the terminal at the project root directory where `GruntFile.js` is located:

```
npm install grunt-contrib-watch
```

The preceding command will install Grunt watch and the `grunt-contrib-watch` directory will be available with the `watch` module.

Now, we will modify this `GruntFile.js` file to add the `watch` module, which will monitor all the files in our defined directories, and if any changes occur, it will run these tasks automatically. This will save a lot of time in manually executing these tasks again and again. Look at the following code; the highlighted code is the modified section:

```
module.exports = function(grunt) {
  /*Load the package.json file*/
  pkg: grunt.file.readJSON('package.json'),
  /*Define Tasks*/
  grunt.initConfig({
    concat: {
      css: {
        src: [
          'css/*' //Load all files in CSS folder
],
        dest: 'dest/combined.css' //Destination of the final combined
file.

      },//End of CSS
js: {
        src: [
          'js/*' //Load all files in js folder
```

```
    ],
          dest: 'dest/combined.js' //Destination of the final combined
    file.

          }, //End of js

  }, //End of concat
  cssmin: {
    css: {
      src : 'dest/combined.css',
      dest : 'dest/combined.min.css'
  }
  }, //End of cssmin
  uglify: {
    js: {
          files: {
          'dest/combined.min.js' : ['dest/combined.js']//destination
    Path : [src path]
  }
  }
  }, //End of uglify

  //The watch starts here
  watch: {
    mywatch: {
      files: ['css/*', 'js/*', 'dist/*'],
      tasks: ['concat', 'cssmin', 'uglify']
    },
  },
  }); //End of initConfig

  grunt.loadNpmTasks('grunt-contrib-watch'); //Include watch module
  grunt.loadNpmTasks('grunt-contrib-concat');
  grunt.loadNpmTasks('grunt-contrib-uglify');
  grunt.loadNpmTasks('grunt-contrib-cssmin');
  grunt.registerTask('default', ['concat:css', 'concat:js',
  'cssmin:css', 'uglify:js']);
  }; //End of module.exports
```

In preceding highlighted code, we added a `watch` block. The `mywatch` title can be any name. The `files` block is required, and it takes an array of the source paths. The Grunt watch watches for changes in these destinations and executes the tasks that are defined in the tasks block. Also, the tasks that are mentioned in the `tasks` block are already created in `GruntFile.js`. Also, we have to load the `watch` module using `grunt.loadNpmTasks`.

Now, open the terminal at the root of the project where `GruntFile.js` is located and run the following command:

```
grunt watch
```

Grunt will start watching the source files for changes. Now, modify any file in the paths defined in the `files` block in `GruntFile.js` and save the file. As soon as the file is saved, the tasks will be executed and the output for the tasks will be displayed in the terminal. A sample output can be seen in the following screenshot:

```
Completed in 0.484s at Sun Apr 03 2016 20:52:35 GMT+0300 (AST) - Waiting...
>> File "dist/combined.js" changed.
>> File "dist/combined.min.css" changed.
>> File "dist/combined.css" changed.
>> File "dist/combined.min.js" changed.
Running "concat:css" (concat) task
File "dist/combined.css" created.

Running "concat:js" (concat) task
File "dist/combined.js" created.

Running "cssmin:css" (cssmin) task
File dist/combined.min.css created.

Running "uglify:js" (uglify) task
File "dist/combined.min.js" created.

Done, without errors.
Completed in 0.519s at Sun Apr 03 2016 20:52:35 GMT+0300 (AST) - Waiting...
```

It is possible to watch as many tasks as required in the `watch` block, but these tasks should be present in `GruntFile.js`.

Summary

In this appendix, we discussed Composer and how to use it to install and update packages. Also, we discussed Git in detail, including pushing, pulling, committing, creating branches, and merging different branches. Also, we discussed Git hooks. Lastly, we discussed Grunt watch and created a watch that executed four tasks whenever any changes occurred in the files paths defined in `GruntFile.js`.

B
MVC and Frameworks

We covered the names of some of the frameworks in different chapters, but we did not discuss them. In today's world, we don't invent the wheel again; we build upon the tools that are already built, tested, and widely used. So, as best practice, if there is nothing available to fulfill the requirements, we can build it using a framework that suits the requirements best.

We will cover the following topics:

- The MVC design pattern
- Laravel
- Lumen
- Apigility

The MVC design pattern

Model View Controller (MVC) is a design pattern widely used in different programming languages. Most PHP frameworks use this design pattern. This pattern divides the application into three layers: Model, View, and Controller. Each one of these has separate tasks, and they are all interconnected. There are different visual representations for MVC, but an overall and simple representation can be seen in the following diagram:

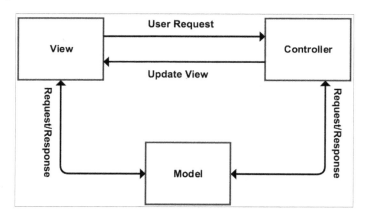

Now, let's discuss each part of the MVC design pattern.

Model

The model layer is the backbone of the application and handles the data logic. Mostly, it is considered that model is responsible for CRUD operations on a database, which may or may not be true. As we mentioned previously, model is responsible for the data logic, which means that data validation operations can also be performed here. In simple words, models provide an abstraction for the data. The remaining application layers don't know or care how and from where the data comes or how an operation is performed on data. It is the model's responsibility to take care of all data logic.

In today's complex framework structures, the overall MVC structure is changed, and not only do models handle data operations, but also, every other application logic is handled by models. The method followed is fat models and slim controllers, which means keep all the application logic in models and the controllers as clean as possible.

Views

Views are what is visible to end users. All data related to this user and public is displayed in the views, so views can be called the visual representation of the models. Views need data to display. It asks for some specific data or action from the controller. Views do not know or want to know from where the controller gets this data; it just asks the controller to get it. Controller knows who to ask for this specific data and communicates with the specific model. It means that views do not have any direct link to models. However, in the earlier diagram, we linked model to view directly. This is because in the advanced systems nowadays, views can directly take data from models. For example, Magento controllers can't send data back to views. For the data (that is, to get data directly from the database) and/or to communicate with models, views communicate with blocks and helper classes. In modern practices, views can be connected to models directly.

Controllers

Controllers respond to actions performed by a user in the views and respond to the view. For example, a user fills a form and submits it. Here, the controller comes in the middle and starts taking action on the submission of the form. Now, the controller will first check whether the user is allowed to make this request or not. Then, the controller will take the appropriate action, such as communicating with the model or any other operation. In a simple analogy, the controller is the middle man between views and models. As we mentioned before in the models section, controllers should be slim. So, mostly, controllers are only used to handle the requests and communicate with models and views. All kinds of data operations are performed in models.

The MVC design pattern's sole job is to separate the responsibilities of different parts in an application. So, models are used to manage the application data. Controllers are used to take actions on user inputs, and views are responsible for the visual representation of data. As we mentioned before, MVC separates the responsibilities of each part, so it does not matter whether it accesses the model from controllers or views; the only thing that matters is that views and controllers should not be used to perform operations on data, as it is the model's responsibility, and controllers should not be used to view any kind of data by the end user as this is the view's responsibility.

Laravel

Laravel is one of the most popular PHP frameworks, and according to the Laravel official website, it is a framework for Web Artisans. Laravel is beautiful, powerful, and has tons of features that can enable developers to write efficient and quality code. The Laravel official documentation is well written and very easy to understand. So, let's play a little with Laravel.

Installation

Installation is very easy and simple. Let's use Composer to install Laravel. We discussed Composer in Appendix A. Issue the following command in the terminal to install and create a project in Laravel:

```
composer create-project --prefer-dist laravel/laravel packt
```

If Composer is not installed globally on the system, place composer.phar in a directory where Laravel should be installed and issue the following command in the terminal at the root of this directory:

```
php composer.phar create-project --prefer-dist laravel/laravel packt
```

Now, Laravel will be downloaded, and a new project with the name packt will be created. Also, Composer will download and install all the dependencies for the project.

Open the browser and head to the project's URL, and we will be welcomed with a nice simple page saying **Laravel 5**.

 As of the writing of this book, Laravel 5.2.29 is the latest version available. However, if Composer is used, then every time the composer update command is used, Laravel and all other components will be automatically updated.

Features

Laravel provides tons of features, and we will only discuss a few here.

Routing

Laravel provides powerful routing. Routes can be grouped, and prefixes, namespaces, and middleware can be defined for route groups. Also, Laravel supports all HTTP methods, including POST, GET, DELETE, PUT, OPTIONS, and PATCH. All the routes are defined in the routes.php file in the application's app folder. Take a look at the following example:

```
Route::group(['prefix' => 'customer', 'namespace' => 'Customer',
  'middleware' => 'web'], function() {
    Route::get('/', 'CustomerController@index');
    Route::post('save', 'CustomerController@save');
    Route::delete('delete/{id}', 'CustomerController@delete');
});
```

In the preceding snippet, we created a new routes group. This will be only used when the URL has a prefixed customer. For example, if a URL is similar to domain. com/customer, this group will be used. We also used a customer namespace. Namespacing allows us to use standard PHP namespaces and divide our files in subfolders. In the preceding example, all customer controllers can be placed in the Customer subfolder in the Controllers directory, and the controller will be created as follows:

```
namespace App\Http\Controllers\Customer

use App\Http\{
Controllers\Controller,
Requests,
};
use Illuminate\Http\Request;

Class CustomerController extends Controller
{
   ...
   ...
}
```

So, namespacing a route group enables us to place our controller files in subfolders, which are easy to manage. Also, we used the web middleware. Middleware provides a way to filter the request before entering the application, which enables us to use it to check whether a user is logged in or not, the CSRF protection, or whether there are any other actions that can be performed in a middleware and need to be performed before the request is sent to application. Laravel comes with a few middleware, including web, api, auth, and so on.

If a route is defined as GET, no POST request can be sent to this route. It is very convenient, which enables us to not worry about the request method filtering. However, HTML forms do not support the HTTP methods like DELETE, PATCH, and PUT. For this, Laravel provides method spoofing, in which a hidden form field with name _method and the value of the HTTP method is used to make this request possible. For example, in our routes group, to make the request possible to delete a route, we need a form similar to the following:

```
<form action="/customer/delete" method="post">
  {{ method_field('DELETE') }}
  {{ csrf_field() }}
</form>
```

When the preceding form is submitted, it will work, and the delete route will be used. Also, we created a CSRF hidden field, which is used for CSRF protection.

 Laravel routing is very interesting, and it is a big topic. More in-depth detail can be found at https://laravel.com/docs/5.2/routing.

Eloquent ORM

Eloquent ORM provides active records to interact with the database. To use Eloquent ORM, we have to just extend our models from the Eloquent model. Let's have a look at a simple user model, as follows:

```
namespace App;

use Illuminate\Database\Eloquent\Model;

class user extends Model
{
  //protected $table = 'customer';
  //protected $primaryKey = 'id_customer';
  ...
  ...
}
```

That's it; we have a model that can handle all the CRUD operations now. Note that we commented the $table property and did the same for $primaryKey. This is because Laravel uses a plural name of the class to look for the table unless the table is defined with the protected $table property. In our case, Laravel will look for table name users and use it. However, if we want to use a table named customers, we can just uncomment the line, as follows:

```
protected $table = 'customers';
```

Similarly, Laravel thinks that a table will have a primary key with the column name id. However, if another column is needed, we can override the default primary key, as follows:

```
protected $primaryKey = 'id_customer';
```

Eloquent models also make it easy for timestamps. By default, if the table has the created_at and updated_at fields, then these two dates will be generated automatically and saved. If no timestamps are required, these can be disabled, as follows:

```
protected $timestamps = false;
```

Saving data to the table is easy. The table columns are used as properties of the models, so if our customer table has columns such as name, email, phone, and so on, we can set them as follows in our customer controller, mentioned in the routing section:

```
namespace App\Http\Controllers\Customer

use App\Http\{
Controllers\Controller,
Requests,
};
use Illuminate\Http\Request;
use App\Customer

Class CustomerController extends Controller
{
  public function save(Request $request)
  {
    $customer = new Customer();
    $customer->name = $request->name;
    $customer->email = $request->email;
    $customer->phone = $request->phone;

    $customer->save();

  }
}
```

In the preceding example, we added the `save` action to our controller. Now, if a POST or GET request is made along the form data, Laravel assigns all the form-submitted data to a Request object as properties with the same names as that of the form fields. Then, using this request object, we can access all the data submitted by the form either using POST or GET. After assigning all the data to model properties (the same names as those of table columns), we can just call the save method. Now, our model does not have any save method, but its parent class, which is the Eloquent model, has this method defined. However, we can override this `save` method in our `model` class in case we need some other features in this method.

Fetching data from the Eloquent model is also easy. Let's try an example. Add a new action to the `customer` controller, as follows:

```
public function index()
{
    $customers = Customer::all();
}
```

We used the `all()` static method in the model, which is basically defined in the Eloquent model, which, in turn, fetches all the data in our `customers` table. Now, if we want to get a single customer by the primary key, we can use the `find($id)` method, as follows:

```
$customer = Customer::find(3);
```

This will fetch the customer with the ID 3.

Updating is simple, and the same `save()` method is used, as shown here:

```
$customer = Customer::find(3);
$customer->name = 'Altaf Hussain';

$customer->save();
```

This will update the customer with the ID 3. First, we loaded the `customer`, then we assigned new data to its properties, and then we called the same `save()` method. Deleting the model is simple and easy and can be done as follows:

```
$customer = Customer::find(3);
$customer->delete();
```

We first loaded the customer with the ID 3, and then we called the `delete` method, which will delete the customer with the ID 3.

Laravel's Eloquent models are very powerful and provide lots of features. These are well explained in the documentation at https://laravel.com/docs/5.2/eloquent. The Laravel database section is also worth reading and can be found at https://laravel.com/docs/5.2/database.

Artisan CLI

Artisan is the command-line interface provided with Laravel, and it has some nice commands that can be used for quicker operations. It has lots of commands, and a full list can be seen using the following command:

```
php artisan list
```

This will list all the options and commands available.

The php artisan command should be run in the same directory in which the artisan file is located. It is placed at the root of the project.

Some of the basic commands are as follows:

- make:controller: This command creates a new controller in the Controllers folder. The command can be used as follows:

  ```
  php artisan make:controller MyController
  ```

  If a namespaced controller is required, as it happened before with the Customer namespace, it can be done as follows:

  ```
  php artisan make:controller Customer/CustomerController
  ```

  This command will create CustomerController in the Customer folder. If the Customer folder is not available, it will create the folder as well.

- make:model: This creates a new model in the app folder. The syntax is the same as the make:controller command, as follows:

  ```
  php artisan make:model Customer
  ```

  For the namespaced models, it can be used as follows:

  ```
  php artisan make:model Customer/Customer
  ```

  This will create the Customer model in the Customer folder and use the Customer namespace for it.

- `make:event`: This creates a new `event` class in the `Events` folder. It can be used as follows:

```
php artisan make:event MyEvent
```

- `make:listener`: This command creates a new listener for an event. This can be used as follows:

```
php artisan make:listener MyListener --event MyEvent
```

  The preceding command will create a new listener for our `MyEvent` event. We have to always mention the event for which we need to create a listener using the `--event` option.

- `make:migration`: This command creates a new migration in the database/migrations folder.

- `php artisan migrate`: This runs all the available migrations that are not executed.

- `php artisan optimize`: This command optimizes the framework for better performance.

- `php artisan down`: This puts the application in maintenance mode.

- `php artisan up`: This command brings the application back live from the maintenance mode.

- `php artisan cache:clear`: This command clears the application cache.

- `php artisan db:seed`: This command seeds the database with records.

- `php artisan view:clear`: This clears all the compiled view files.

 More detail about the Artisan console or Artisan CLI can be found in the documentation at `https://laravel.com/docs/5.2/homestead`.

Migrations

Migrations is another powerful feature in Laravel. In migrations, we define the database schemas—whether it creates tables, removes tables, or adds/updates columns in the tables. Migrations are very convenient in deployment and act as version control for the database. Let's create a migration for our customer table that is not available in the database yet. To create a migration, issue the following command in the terminal:

```
php artisan make:migration create_custmer_table
```

A new file in the `database/migrations` folder will be created with the filename `create_customer_table` prefixed with the current date and a unique ID. The class is created as `CreateCustomerTable`. This is a class as follows:

```
use Illuminate\Database\Schema\Blueprint;
use Illuminate\Database\Migrations\Migration;

class CreateCustomerTable extends Migrations
{
  //Run the migrations

  public function up()
  {
    //schemas defined here
  }

  public function down()
  {
    //Reverse migrations
  }
}
```

The class will have two public methods: `up()` and `down()`. The `up()` method should have all the new schemas for the table(s). The `down()` method is responsible for reversing the executed migration. Now, lets add the `customers` table schema to the `up()` method, as follows:

```
public function up()
{
  Schema::create('customers', function (Blueprint $table)
  {
    $table->increments('id', 11);
    $table->string('name', 250)
    $table->string('email', 50);
    $table->string('phone', 20);
    $table->timestamps();
  });
}
public function down()
{
  Schema::drop('customers');
}
```

In the `up()` method, we defined the schema and table name. Columns for the table are individually defined, including the column size. The `increments()` method defines the autoincrement column, which, in our case, is the `id` column. Next, we created three string columns for `name`, `email`, and `phone`. Then, we used the `timestamps()` method, which creates the `created_at` and `updated_at` timestamp columns. In the `down()` method, we just used the `drop()` method of the `Schema` class to drop out the `customers` table. Now, we need to run our migrations using the following command:

```
php artisan migrate
```

The preceding command will not only run our migration but will also run all those migrations that are not executed yet. When a migration is executed, Laravel stores the migration name in a table called `migrations`, from where Laravel decides which migrations it has to execute and which to skip.

Now, if we need to roll back the latest executed migration, we can use the following command:

```
php artisan migrate:rollback
```

This will roll back to the last batch of migrations. To roll back all the migrations of the application, we can use the reset command, as follows:

```
php artisan migrate:reset
```

This will roll back the complete application migrations.

Migrations make it easy for deployment because we won't need to upload the database schemas every time we create some new changes in the tables or database. We will just create the migrations and upload all the files, and after this, we will just execute the migration command, and all the schemas will be updated.

Blade templates

Laravel comes with its own template language called Blade. Also, Blade template files support plain PHP code. Blade template files are compiled to plain PHP files and are cached until they are changed. Blade also supports layouts. For example, the following is our master page layout in Blade, placed in the `resources/views/layout` folder with the name `master.blade.php`. Take a look at the following code:

```html
<!DOCTYPE html>
<html>
  <head>
    <title>@yield('title')</title>
  </head>
```

```
<body>
  @section('sidebar')
    Our main sidebar
  @show

  <div class="contents">
    @yield('content')
  </div>
</body>
</html>
```

In the preceding example, we had a section for the sidebar that defines a content section. Also, we had @yield, which displays the contents of a section. Now, if we want to use this layout, we will need to extend it in the child template files. Let's create the customers.blade.php file in the resources/views/ folder and place the following code in it:

```
@extend('layouts.master')
  @section('title', 'All Customers')
  @section('sidebar')
  This will be our side bar contents
  @endsection
  @section('contents')
    These will be our main contents of the page
  @endsection
```

As can be seen in the preceding code, we extended the master layout and then placed contents in every section of the master layout. Also, it is possible to include different templates in another template. For example, let's have two files, sidebar.blade.php and menu.blade.php, in the resources/views/includes folder. Then, we can include these files in any template, as follows:

```
@include(includes.menu)
@include(includes.sidebar)
```

We used @include to include a template. The dot (.) indicates a folder separation. We can easily send data to Blade templates or views from our controllers or routers. We have to just pass the data as an array to a view, as follows:

```
return view('customers', ['count => 5]);
```

Now, count is available in our customers view file and can be accessed as follows:

```
Total Number of Customers: {{ count }}
```

Yes, Blade uses double curly braces to echo a variable. For control structures and loops, let's have another example. Let's send data to the `customers` view, as follows:

```
return view('customers', ['customers' => $allCustomers]);
```

Now, our `customers` view file will be similar to the following if we want to display all the `customers` data:

```
...
...
@if (count($customers) > 0)
{{ count($customers) }} found. <br />
@foreach ($customers as $customer)
{{ $customer->name }} {{ $customer->email }}
  {{ $customer->phone }} <br>
@endforeach

@else
Now customers found.
@endif;
...
...
```

All the preceding syntax looks familiar as it is almost the same as plain PHP. However, to display a variable, we have to use double curly braces {{}}.

 A nice and easy-to-read documentation for Blade templates can be found at https://laravel.com/docs/5.2/blade.

Other features

We only discussed a few basic features in the previous section. Laravel has tons of other features, such as Authentication and Authorization, which provide an easy way to authenticate and authorize users. Also, Laravel provides a powerful caching system, which supports file-based cache, the Memcached, and Redis cache. Laravel also provides events and listeners for these events, which is very convenient when we want to perform a specific action and when a specific event occurs. Laravel supports localization, which enables us to use localized contents and multiple languages. Laravel also supports task scheduling and queues, in which we schedule some tasks to run at a specific time and queue some tasks to be run when their turn arrives.

Lumen

Lumen is a micro-framework provided by Laravel. Lumen is mainly intended to create stateless APIs and has a minimal set of features of Laravel. Also, Lumen is compatible with Laravel, which means that if we just copy our Lumen application to Laravel, it will work fine. The installation is simple. Just use the following Composer command to create a Lumen project, and it will download all the dependencies, including Lumen:

```
composer create-project --prefer-dist laravel/lumen api
```

The preceding command will download Lumen and then create our API application. After this, rename .env.example as .env. Also, create a 32-characters-long app key and place it in the .env file. Now, the basic application is ready to use and create APIs.

 Lumen is almost the same as Laravel, but some Laravel features are not included by default. More details can be found at https://lumen. laravel.com/docs/5.2.

Apigility

Apigility is built and developed by Zend in Zend Framework 2. Apigility provides an easy to use GUI to create and manage APIs. It is very easy to use and is capable of creating complex APIs. Let's start by installing Apigility using Composer. Issue the following command in the terminal:

```
composer create-project -sdev zfcampus/zf-apigility-skeleton packt
```

The preceding command will download Apigility and its dependencies, including Zend Framework 2, and will set up our project named packt. Now, issue the following command to enable the development mode so that we can have access to the GUI:

```
php public/index.php development enable
```

Now, open the URL as `yourdomain.com/packt/public`, and we will see a beautiful GUI, as shown in the following screenshot:

Now, let's create our first API. We will call this API "`books`", which will return a list of books. Click on the **New API** button, as shown in the preceding picture, and a popup will be displayed. In the text box, enter `books` as the API name and click on `Create` button; the new API will be created. When the API is created, we will be presented with the following screen:

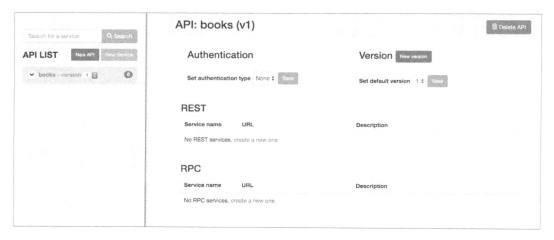

Apigility provides easy ways to set other properties for the API, such as versioning and authentication. Now, let's create an RPC service by clicking on the **New Service** button in the left sidebar. Also, we can click on the **Create a new one** link in the **RPC** section in the preceding screenshot. We will be presented with the following screen:

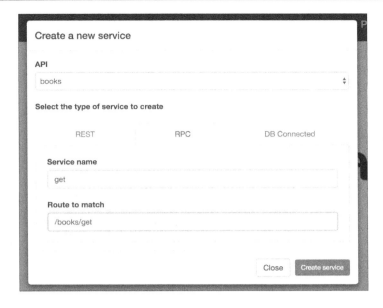

As shown in the preceding screenshot, we created an RPC service named `get` in the `books` API. The route URI entered is `/books/get`, which will be used to call this RPC service. When we click on the `Create service` button, the API creation successful message will be displayed, and also, the following screen will be displayed:

As can be seen in the preceding screenshot, the allowed HTTP method for this service is only **GET**. Let's keep this as it is, but we can select all or any of them. Also, we want to keep **Content Negotiation Selector** as Json, and our service will accept/receive all the content in the JSON format. Also, we can select different media types and content types.

Next, we should add some fields to our service that will be used. Click on the **Fields** tab, and we will see the **Fields** screen. Click on the **New Field** button, and we will be presented with the following popup:

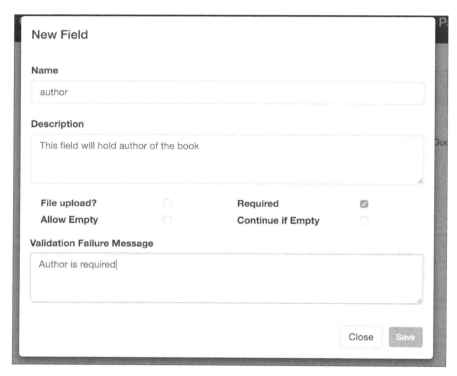

As can be seen in the preceding screenshot, we can set all the properties for a field, such as the **Name**, **Description**, whether it is required or not, and some other settings, including an error message if the validation fails. After we created two fields, **title** and **author**, we will have a screen similar to the following:

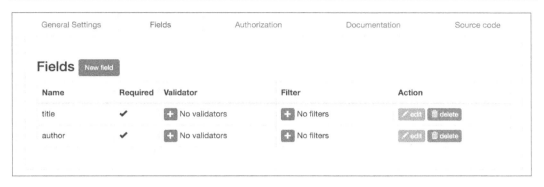

As can be seen in the preceding screen, we can add validators and filters to each individual field too.

 As this is just an introductory topic for Apigility, we will not cover validators and filters and some other topics in this book.

The next topic is documentation. When we click on the **Documentation** tab, we will see the following screen:

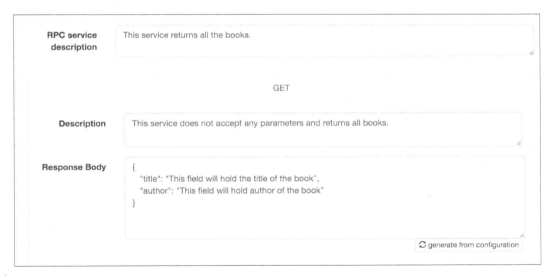

Here, we will document our service, add some description, and also can generate the response body for documentation purposes. This is very important as it will enable others to better understand our APIs and services.

Now, we need to get the all the books from somewhere. It can be either from the database or from another service or any other source. However, for now, we will just use an array of books for test purposes. If we click on the **Source** tab, we will find that our code for the service is placed at `module/books/src/books/V1/Rpc/ Get/GetController.php`. Apigility created a module for our API `books` and then placed all the source code in this module in different folders according to the version of our API, which is V1 by default. We can add more versions, such as V2 and V3, to our APIs. Now, if we open the `GetController` file, we will find some code and an action called `getAction` according to our route URI. The code is as follows, and the highlighted code is the one we added:

```php
namespace books\V1\Rpc\Get;

use Zend\Mvc\Controller\AbstractActionController;
use ZF\ContentNegotiation\ViewModel;


class GetController extends AbstractActionController
{
  public function getAction()
  {
    $books = [ 'success' => [
    [
      'title' => 'PHP 7 High Performance',
      'author' => 'Altaf Hussain'
    ],
    [
      'title' => 'Magento 2',
      'author' => 'Packt Publisher'
    ],
    ]
    ];

    return new ViewModel($books);
  }
}
```

In the preceding code, we used `ContentNegotiation\ViewModel`, which is responsible for responding with the data in the format that we selected in the service setup, which is JSON in our case. Then, we created a simple `$books` array with the fieldnames we created for the service and assigned our values to them. Then, we returned them using the `ViewModel` object, which handles the response data conversion to JSON.

Now, let's test our API. As our service can accept GET requests, we will just type our URL in the browser with the books/get URI, and we will see the JSON response. It is best to check the API with tools such as RestClient or Postman for Google Chrome, which provides an easy-to-use interface to make different types of requests to APIs. We tested it with Postman and got the response shown in the following screenshot:

```
Body      Cookies    Headers (7)    Tests

Pretty    Raw     Preview      JSON  ∨   ⇉

 1 ▾ {
 2 ▾    "success": [
 3 ▾       {
 4            "title": "PHP 7 High Performance",
 5            "author": "Altaf Hussain"
 6         },
 7 ▾       {
 8            "title": "Magento 2",
 9            "author": "Packt Publisher"
10         }
11      ]
12  }
```

Also note that we set our service to accept only GET requests. So, if we send a request other than GET, we will get an HTTP Status code 405 methods not allowed error.

Apigility is very powerful and provides tons of features, such as RESTFul APIs, HTTP authentication, database connected services with easy-to-create DB connectors, and a selection of tables for a service. While using Apigility, we need not worry about the API, service structure security, and other things, as Apigility does this for us. We need to only concentrate on the business logic of the APIs and services.

Apigility can't be covered completely in this Appendix. Apigility has lots of features that can be covered in a complete book. Apigility's official documentation at https://apigility.org/documentation is a good place to get started and read more about this.

Summary

In this Appendix, we discussed the basics of the MVC design pattern. We also discussed the Laravel framework and some of its good features. We introduced you to the Laravel-based micro-framework, Lumen. At the end, we had a small introduction to Apigility and created a test API and web service.

In IT, things get obsolete in a very short time span. It is always required to study upgraded tools and find new ways and techniques for the best approaches in programming. Therefore, one should not stop after completing this book and start studying new topics and also the topics that are not covered completely in this book. Until this point, you will have the knowledge that you can use to set up high-performance environments for high-performance applications. We wish you good luck and success in PHP-ing!

Index

A

anonymous classes 27-30
Apache 42
ApacheBench (ab) 120, 121
Apache JMeter
  about 114-119
  reference link 114
Apigility
  about 169-175
  reference link 175
Artisan CLI, Laravel
  about 163
  make:controller command 163
  make:event command 164
  make:listener command 164
  make:migration command 164
  make:model command 163
  php artisan cache:clear command 164
  php artisan db:seed command 164
  php artisan down command 164
  php artisan migrate command 164
  php artisan optimize command 164
  php artisan up command 164
  php artisan view:clear command 164
  reference link 164

B

base collectors 111
best practices, PHP Programming
  coding styles 130
  Continuous Integration (CI) 138
  deployment 138
  design patterns 136
  Git 138
  object-oriented 137
  PHP frameworks 138
  reusable feature 137
  service-oriented architecture (SOA) 137
  test-driven development (TDD) 133
  version control system (VCS) 138
Blade templates, Laravel
  about 166, 168
  reference link 168

C

coding styles 130-132
Community Enterprise Operating System
      (CentOS)
  NGINX, installing 10
  Percona Server, installing 13
  PHP 7, installing 11, 12
  setting up 9
Composer
  about 141
  dependencies, download link 141
  installation 142
  reference link 108
  using 142, 143
Content Delivery Network (CDN)
  about 52
  features 52
  reference links 53
  using 52, 53
Continuous Integration (CI) 138-140
Create Read Update Delete (CRUD) 136
CSS and JavaScript optimization
  about 54
  Grunt 58-62
  merging process 54

Minify 56-58
minifying process 54, 55

D

Debian
about 5
setting up 5
debugging
with Eclipse 102-105
with Sublime Text 98-102
deployment
about 139, 140
setup 139
design patterns 136
development environment
CentOS, setting up 9
Debian, setting up 5
Ubuntu, setting up 5
Vagrant, setting up 14
Windows, setting up 2
Drupal 8 127

E

Eclipse
used, for debugging 102-105
eloquent ORM, Laravel
about 160-162
reference link 163

F

FLUSHALL command 91
FLUSHDB command 91
full page caching 62

G

Git
about 138, 144
desktop tools, used for managing
repositories 150, 151
installation 144
new branches, creating 146, 147
new branches, merging 146, 147
reference link 138

repository, cloning 148
using 144-146
webhooks 148, 149
GitHub Desktop
download link 150
group use declaration
about 21-25
compound namespace declaration 26
mixed group use declarations 26
non mixed group use declarations 25
Grunt
about 58
reference link 62
Grunt watch 151-154
GZIP compression
about 46
in Apache 46, 47
in NGINX 47, 48

H

HAProxy
installation 68, 69
load balancing 68-72
Homestead Vagrant box
reference link 98
HTTP persistent connection
about 44
benefits 44, 45
GZIP compression 46
in Apache 45
in NGINX 46
PHP, using as separate service 48
unused modules, disabling 49
web server resources 51
HTTP server optimization
about 43
static files, caching 43

I

infrastructure
about 66, 67
database server 67
HAProxy, load balancing 68
load balancer (LB) 67, 68
web servers 67

InnoDB storage engine
  features 77
  innodb_buffer_pool_instances 77
  innodb_buffer_pool_size 77
  innodb_log_file_size 78
installation
  Composer 142
  Git 144
  Percona Server 78, 79

J

Just In Time (JIT) 1

K

KEYS command 91

L

Laravel
  about 158
  Artisan 163
  Artisan CLI 164
  Blade templates 166-168
  eloquent ORM 160-162
  features 158, 168
  installation 158
  migrations 164, 166
  reference link 160
  routing 159
Lumen
  about 169
  reference link 169

M

Magento 2 125
Memcached
  key-value cache store 95, 96
Minify
  reference links 56
Model View Controller (MVC)
    design pattern
  about 156
  controllers 157
  model layer 156, 157

MyISAM storage engine
  features 76
MySQL database
  about 73
  query caching 74, 75
MySQL performance monitoring tools
  about 79
  MySQL workbench 83
  Percona Toolkit 84
  phpMyAdmin 80-83
MySQL workbench 83

N

NGINX
  about 41, 42
  installing 10
NGINX Windows binaries
  download link 2
null coalesce operator(??) 36

O

OOP features
  about 18
  anonymous classes 27-30
  group use declaration 21
  namespaces 21
  old-style constructor deprecation 30, 31
  throwable interface 32
  type hints 18
operators, PHP
  about 33
  null coalesce operator(??) 35, 36
  Spaceship operator (<=>) 33-35

P

packt-git
  reference link 144
path converter library
  download link 56
Percona Server
  about 78
  installing 13, 78, 79
  reference link 78

Percona Toolkit
  about 84
  pt-duplicate-key-checker 85, 86
  pt-query-digest 84
  reference link 84
Percona XtraDB Cluster (PXC) 87-89
PHP 7
  about 1, 17
  installing 11, 12
PHP 7, features
  about 38
  constant arrays 38
  filtered unserialize function 39
  multiple default cases, in switch
     statement 38
  OOP features 18
  operators 33
  session_start function, options array 39
  uniform variable syntax 37
PHP DebugBar
  about 107-111
  reference link 111
PHP Framework Interop Group (PHP-FIG)
  about 130
  reference link 130
PHP frameworks 138
phpMyAdmin 80-83
PHP next generation (PHPng) 1
PHPRedis
  reference link 91
PHPUnit
  reference link 133
PHP Windows binaries
  download link 2
profiling
  with Xdebug 106
PuPHPet
  reference link 4
PuTTY
  download link 15

Q

query caching
  enabling 74, 75

R

real-world applications, load testing
  about 124
  Drupal 8 127
  Magento 2 125
  WordPress 4 126
Redis
  about 89-91
  connecting, with server 92
  data, fetching 92, 93
  data, storing 92, 93
  features 94
  installation link 89
  management tools 94
  reference link 89
Redis Desktop Manager (RDM) 94
Relational Database Management System
  (RDMS) 73

S

SELECT command 91
service-oriented architecture (SOA) 137
session_start function 39
Siege
  about 122-124
  reference link 124
singleton pattern 136
Spaceship operator (<=>) 33-35
  reference link 34
State Snapshot Transfer (SST) 88
static files
  Apache configuration 43
  caching 43
  NGINX 43, 44
storage engines
  about 75, 76
  InnoDB storage engine 77
  MyISAM storage engine 76
  reference link 76
Sublime Text
  used, for debugging 98-102

T

test-driven development (TDD) 133-135
throwable interface
  about 32
  error 32, 33
type hints
  about 18
  return type hints 19-21
  scala type hints 18, 19

U

Ubuntu
  about 5
  setting up 5-9
Uncaught Type Error 19
uniform variable syntax
  about 37, 38
  null coalesce operator(??) 36-38
unserialize() function 39
unused modules
  disabling 49
  disabling, in Apache 49, 50
  disabling, in NGINX 50

V

Vagrant
  about 4
  download link 14
  setting up 14, 15
Varnish
  about 63-65
  reference link 65
version control system (VCS) 138

W

web server resources
  about 51
  in NGINX 51
Windows
  setting up 2-4
WordPress 4 126

X

Xdebug
  about 97, 98
  used, for profiling 106, 107

Z

Zend Engine 1
Zend Framework 2 130